Social Issues
in Literature

Colonialism in
Chinua Achebe's
Things Fall Apart

Other Books in the Social Issues in Literature Series:

Social Issues
in Literature

Colonialism in Chinua Achebe's *Things Fall Apart*

Louise Hawker, Book Editor

GREENHAVEN PRESS
A part of Gale, Cengage Learning

GALE
CENGAGE Learning

Detroit • New York • San Francisco • New Haven, Conn • Waterville, Maine • London

GALE
CENGAGE Learning™

Christine Nasso, *Publisher*
Elizabeth Des Chenes, *Managing Editor*

© 2010 Greenhaven Press, a part of Gale, Cengage Learning

For more information, contact:
Greenhaven Press
27500 Drake Rd.
Farmington Hills, MI 48331-3535
Or you can visit our Internet site at gale.cengage.com

For product information and technology assistance, contact us at

Gale Customer Support, 1-800-877-4253
For permission to use material from this text or product, submit all requests online at www.cengage.com/permissions

Further permissions questions can be emailed to permissionrequest@cengage.com

Articles in Greenhaven Press anthologies are often edited for length to meet page requirements. In addition, original titles of these works are changed to clearly present the main thesis and to explicitly indicate the author's opinion. Every effort is made to ensure that Greenhaven Press accurately reflects the original intent of the authors. Every effort has been made to trace the owners of copyrighted material.

Cover image © Frank May/Corbis.

LIBRARY OF CONGRESS CATALOGING-IN-PUBLICATION DATA

Colonialism in Chinua Achebe's Things fall apart / Louise Hawker, book editor.
    p. cm. -- (Social issues in literature)
  Includes bibliographical references and index.
  ISBN 978-0-7377-4650-1 (hardcover) -- ISBN 978-0-7377-4651-8 (pbk.)
  1. Achebe, Chinua. Things fall apart. 2. Colonies in literature. 3. Imperialism in literature. 4. Nigeria--In literature. I. Hawker, Louise.
  PR9387.9.A3T523975 2010
  823'.914--dc22
                                                          2009048147

Printed in the United States of America
1 2 3 4 5 6 7 14 13 12 11 10

Contents

Even before the colonial rule directly impacts Okonkwo's world, he betrays African and Igbo tradition in beliefs such as the hatred of his father's way of life. Okonkwo becomes increasingly alienated from the beliefs that are the signature of his culture.

The Igbo must search for values in a world that is constantly changing. The cycle of history is evident in both the African and European traditions. The Igbo traditions are clearly presented in the first sections of the book. As the novel draws to a close, Okonkwo tries in vain to defend his tribe's values against Western influences.

Chapter 3: Contemporary Perspectives on Colonialism

Introduction

Chinua Achebe is many things—a consummate storyteller, an advocate for his country of origin, an observer of a nation in transition, and an outspoken critic of Nigeria's post-colonial government. Above all, he is African. These elements of his life have commingled and combined to position Achebe as the first voice—some consider him the grandfather—of modern African literature. The driving force behind Achebe's work has been to portray his people and heritage realistically—to free Nigeria and Africa from the romanticized and sentimental stereotypes and purely erroneous portrayals of their cultures promoted by other writers. His impact and influence on African literature and society cannot be underestimated. Since its publication in 1958, *Things Fall Apart* has sold more than 12 million copies and been translated into fifty languages.

The literature that Achebe encountered as a young man provided his first inkling that the African continent and its tribal cultures had not been accurately represented. Even well-meaning authors perpetuated the European perspective of the African milieu. Achebe has stated that *Mister Johnson*, a novel by English writer Joyce Cary, set in Nigeria, was his first inspiration to become a writer. Achebe has been quoted as saying that "in spite of [Cary's] sympathy and understanding, he could not get under the skin of his African." Numerous other European writers, many of them English, wrote novels during the period of colonization that did not reflect as benign an intent as Cary's work. Many of these novels intentionally played on stereotypes of Africa. Because they were also the product of the colonizers, the novels presented a one-sided view. Many years later, Achebe argued that Joseph Conrad's classic novella *Heart of Darkness* contained racist stereotypes. The criticism inspired widespread debate.

In light of inaccurate depictions in many works about Africa, Achebe has felt it his duty as an artist and social commentator to teach Africans about the real life of the Igbo, his people, and to encourage them to honor the value of their heritage. At the same time, he has sought to undo the damage done to his people and all Africans by making his stories accessible and deceptively simple for a wide range of readers. To Achebe and his Africa, the artist and society are one, unlike the prevalent Western perception of art as something apart from everyday life. He believes that an African writer who tries to remain separate from social and political issues becomes irrelevant.

Throughout his writing career Achebe has demonstrated his commitment to active engagement in African, and specifically Nigerian, issues. His commentary does not end with his novels. In the mid-1960s Nigeria experienced its first military coup, which included persecution of Igbo people. Achebe returned to his homeland upon learning of a genocide occurring there. Soon after, the state of Biafra declared its independence from Nigeria. Biafra gained notoriety for its post-independence famine and need for international aid. Achebe represented Biafra and its struggle for independence to Europe and the United States throughout its civil war. In fact, Achebe did not write any novels between 1966 and 1988, preferring instead to focus his energies on Biafra's struggle for independence.

In the early 1980s Achebe became an active participant in Nigerian party politics. In 1983 he published *The Trouble with Nigeria*, which reflected his view of the postcolonial failures of the Nigerian government. He has not hesitated to point out what he believes are the shortcomings that still haunt the "new" Nigeria.

Achebe remains an important voice in Africa. In 2009 he published his first book in more than twenty years. Titled *The Education of a British-Protected Child*, the book is an autobiographical collection of essays that cover his many years in the literary profession. In these essays his life and the life of Nigeria remain interwoven. Achebe has also served to inspire new generations of African writers.

Achebe's appointment in 2009 to the faculty of Brown University in Rhode Island includes the launch of the Chinua Achebe Colloquium on Africa. This new program, to be developed by Achebe, aligns with his life's mission to foster greater understanding of Africa.

More than fifty years after its publication, *Things Fall Apart* stands as the most widely read novel of African fiction. And Achebe's dedication to his role as educator and teacher about the real Africa and its people is as fervent as ever.

Chronology

1930
Chinua Achebe is born in Ogidi, Nigeria, to Isaiah Okafo and Janet N. Iloegbuman Achebe.

1938
Achebe begins to learn English.

1944
Achebe is chosen to attend the Government College at Umuahia, Nigeria.

1948
Achebe enrolls in University College, Ibadan, Nigeria.

1953
Achebe graduates from University College with a bachelor of arts degree.

1954
Achebe takes a job at the Nigerian Broadcasting Service and becomes a talk show producer.

1956
Achebe studies broadcasting at the British Broadcasting Corporation, London.

1958
Things Fall Apart, Achebe's first novel, is published.

1960
Achebe publishes his second novel, *No Longer at Ease*, dedicated to Christiana Chinwe Okoli, whom he met while working at the Nigerian Broadcasting Service.

Achebe receives a Rockefeller Fellowship for six months of travel and tours East Africa.

1961

Achebe marries Christiana Chinwe Okoli.

1962

The Achebes' first child, daughter Chinelo, is born.

Achebe travels to the United States on a UNESCO Fellowship for Creative Artists

1964

Arrow of God, Achebe's third novel, is published.

The Achebes' second child, son Ikechukwu, is born.

1966

A Man of the People, Achebe's fourth novel, is published.

Chike and the River, his first children's book, is published.

1967

The Achebes' third child, son Chidi, is born.

Biafra, the southeastern region of Nigeria, secedes and forms the Republic of Biafra; civil war ensues.

1970

The Achebes' fourth child, daughter Nwando, is born.

The independence of Biafra ends; Achebe's passport is revoked as a result of his Biafran support.

Achebe accepts a position at the University of Nigeria.

1971

Achebe publishes his poetry collection, *Beware Soul Brother*, while living in a Biafran war zone.

1972

The short story collection, *Girls at War*, is published.

Achebe accepts a professorship at the University of Massachusetts, Amherst, and the family moves to the United States.

1975

Achebe criticizes Joseph Conrad's novel *Heart of Darkness* in a lecture at Amherst.

1976

Achebe returns to the University of Nigeria.

1982

Achebe retires from the University of Nigeria.

1983

Achebe becomes deputy national vice president of the People's Redemption Party and publishes his book *The Trouble with Nigeria*.

1986

Achebe is elected president-general of the Ogidi Town Union.

1987

Anthills of the Savannah, Achebe's fifth novel, is published.

1990

Achebe is involved in a car accident en route to Lagos and is permanently paralyzed from the waist down.

1993

Achebe joins the faculty of Bard College, Annandale-on-Hudson, New York.

2000

A collection of autobiographical essays, *Home and Exile*, is published.

2007

Achebe wins the Man Booker International Prize for Fiction in honor of his literary career.

2009

After almost two decades away from his native land, Achebe returns to Nigeria to deliver a lecture.

Achebe joins the faculty of Brown University in Providence, Rhode Island.

October 2009

The Education of a British-Protected Child is published.

Social Issues
in Literature

Background on
Chinua Achebe

The Life of Chinua Achebe

G.D. Killam

G.D. Killam has written extensively on African literature, with special emphasis on the works of Chinua Achebe. He is University Professor Emeritus in the School of English and Theatre Studies at the University of Guelph, Canada, where he formerly was professor of Commonwealth and African Literature. He has also taught in several African nations.

In the following selection, Killam asserts that Achebe established a new voice for African writers with his ground-breaking novel, Things Fall Apart. *Achebe's life experiences, his appreciation for the history of his people, and his political viewpoint coalesced in a work of fiction that portrays Africa and Africans realistically, rather than in the patronizing model promoted by earlier authors. Killam points out that even as Achebe wrote about the "real" Africa, he was influenced by his boyhood as the son of a Christian missionary. In more recent years, Killam explains, Achebe has assumed the role of a spokesman for his native Nigeria and has publicly commented on its postcolonial political struggles.*

Chinua Achebe is arguably the most discussed African writer of his generation. His first novel, *Things Fall Apart* (1958), has become a classic. It has been read and discussed by readers throughout the anglophone [English-speaking] world and has been translated into some forty languages. Sales are estimated to be in excess of three million copies. His other novels—*No Longer at Ease* (1960), *Arrow of God* (1964), *A Man of the People* (1966), and *Anthills of the Savannah* (1987)—are equally respected. A substantial body of scholarship and criticism has grown up around each of these books.

G.D. Killam, "Chinua Achebe," in *Dictionary of Literary Biography, vol. 117, Twentieth-Century Caribbean and Black African Writers, First Series*, edited by Bernth Lindfors and Reinhard Sander, Detroit, MI: The Gale Group, 1992, pp. 15–34. Copyright © 1992 by Gale. Reproduced by permission of Gale, a part of Cengage Learning.

Achebe was born on 16 November 1930 in the village of Ogidi in eastern Nigeria. His mother was Janet Iloegbunam Achebe. His father, Isaiah Okafor Achebe, was a catechist for the Church Missionary Society, and the young Achebe's primary education was in the society's school in Ogidi. He was eight when he began to learn English and fourteen when he went, as one of the few boys selected, to the Government College at Umuahia, one of the best schools in West Africa. He enrolled in 1948 at University College, Ibadan, as a member of the first class to attend this new school. He intended to study medicine but soon switched to English literary studies and followed a syllabus that almost exactly resembled the University of London honors degree program, Ibadan's college being then a constituent college of the University of London. He contributed stories, essays, and sketches to the *University Herald.* (The stories were published in 1972 in *Girls at War and Other Stories.*) After graduating in 1953 he firmly decided to be a writer.

Achebe is a master of the craft of fiction; he has extended the capability of English beyond the limits it had achieved to the point when he published his first novel. His control of language is absolute, and his wide range of usage is appropriate to the multiplicity of his interests.

Things Fall Apart first received attention, however, because of the social purposes he assigned to it and to himself as writer. The novel was published two years before Nigerian independence was gained in 1960. The timing was superb: while Africans—Nigerians in this case—looked forward with excitement and optimism to the political freedom they would attain after more than a half century of colonial rule, Achebe understood the necessity of showing his countrymen the strength of their own cultures to assist in the task of nation building, a strength greatly diminished by the imposition of an alien culture: "as far as I am concerned the fundamental theme ... is that African people did not hear of culture for the first time from Europeans; that their societies were not mindless but frequently had a philosophy of great depth and value and beauty, that they had poetry and, above all, they had dignity. It is this dignity that African people all but lost during the colonial period, and it is this that they must now regain."

Achebe Writes for and about Igbos

Interested in stories and storytelling since his youth, Achebe had his interest in becoming a writer confirmed when he encountered Joyce Cary's novel *Mister Johnson* (1939): "one of the things that probably finally decided me was a novel set in Nigeria . . . called *Mister Johnson*, which is quite famous, and I feel that . . . in spite of [Cary's] ability, in spite of his sympathy and understanding, he could not get under the skin of his African. They just did not communicate. And I felt if a good writer could make this mess perhaps we ought to try our hand." For Achebe, the character Mister Johnson represents the worst kind of presentation of Africans by Europeans, the more so because Cary was working hard at getting the presentation right and not writing fiction that deliberately, often cynically, exploited the stereotypes of Africans and African society that informed the hundreds of novels written by Englishmen about Africa during the imperial-colonial period. It was precisely because Cary was a liberal-minded and sympathetic writer, as well as a colonial administrator, that Achebe felt the record had to be set straight.

Achebe's purpose, then, is to write about his own people and for his own people. His five novels to date form a continuum of time over some one hundred years of Igbo civilization. Europeans have not yet penetrated Umuofia, the setting of the first novel, when this period begins. When it ends, colonial rule has been established, significant change has taken place, and the character of the community—its values and freedoms—have been substantially and irrevocably altered. *Arrow of God*, his third novel, has much the same setting as

Things Fall Apart with the difference that colonial rule has been consolidated and the lives of the villagers are completely circumscribed by it. The action of *No Longer at Ease* (his second novel) takes place in the period immediately before independence from British colonial rule in Nigeria; *A Man of the People* and *Anthills of the Savannah* are located in unspecified African countries (strongly resembling Nigeria) in the immediate postindependence period. The novels therefore form an imaginative history of a segment of a major group of people in what eventually became Nigeria, as seen from the perspective of a Christian Igboman.

Christian Influences

Achebe has said in various places that the fact of his Christian upbringing was important in his evolution as a writer. The Christian rituals, which shaped his upbringing, he later detected in the Igbo religion itself, and it is this recognition that has shaped his art and might be said to be a controlling metaphor of it. He writes, in the introduction to *African Short Stories* (1985): "The Igbo world is an arena for the interplay of forces. It is a dynamic world of movement and flux. . . . In some cultures an individual may worship one of the gods or goddesses in the pantheon and pay scant attention to the rest. In Igbo religion such selectiveness would be unthinkable. All the people must placate all the gods all the time! For there is a cautionary proverb which states that even when a person has satisfied Udo completely he may be killed by Ogwugwu! The degree of peril propounded by this proverb is only dimly apprehended until one realises that Ogwugwu is Udo's loving consort."

Given Achebe's purposes as an artist—the duty to the art and the social purposes he has said he means it to serve—one can say that his is a distinctly Igbo sensibility. His art reflects in all its variety the endless permutations of the essential duality of Igbo life. The connection between this worldview and artistic irony is, of course, apparent. Achebe's art is essentially an art of irony, from the simple to the profound. What makes Achebe's irony different from that of writers from purely literary cultures is that, while their uses of irony are cultivated, his is instinctive, generating as it does from the substance of his culture and being inseparable from it.

Seeking Igbo History and Philosophy

There was a five-year gap between the publication of his stories in the university paper and the release of *Things Fall Apart*. In that interval Achebe taught for a year and then embarked on a twelve-year career as a producer for the Nigerian Broadcasting Corporation. In 1957 he went to London to attend the British Broadcasting Corporation Staff School. One of his teachers there was the British novelist and literary critic Gilbert Phelps. Phelps recognized the quality of *Things Fall Apart* and recommended it for publication. Achebe has remarked that he never had to endure the experience of the struggling artist.

There are other related reasons why there was a gap between the stories of student days and the publication of *Things Fall Apart*. There was the purely practical reason of finding time to write in the midst of a full professional life. He was appointed director of the Voice of Nigeria (external broadcasting) by the Nigerian Broadcasting Corporation in 1961. That same year, on 10 September, he married Christie Chinwe Okoli and became involved in domesticity. But some reasons were more profound. Having determined that one of his purposes was essentially a political one—to set straight the record propounded about Nigerian life by Europeans—he had to find out in more detail than he knew at the time what the native philosophy was and what the basis was for its depth and value and beauty. More than that, and most difficult and elusive in accounting for, he had to discover the appropriate form and language for his fictional evocations.

As Achebe admits, he largely "picked up" the history of his society: "this was the life that interested me, partly the life I lived and the life that was lived around me, supported by what I heard in conversation—I was very keen on listening to old people—and what I learned from my father, so it was sort of picked up here and there. There was no research in the library. . . ." But Achebe was aware of and read the writing of colonial administrators and missionaries, especially the quasi-anthropological treatises of G.T. Basden, who was a close friend of Achebe's father. (Basden performed the wedding ceremony for Achebe's parents and was honored by Achebe's village, Ogidi, with a carved tusk.) Like Cary's, presumably Basden's heart was in the right place, and it was precisely because he was sincere and earnest that his woefully wrong-headed interpretations of Igbo customs could not go unchallenged. He was ineluctably [inevitably] one of those who, through his writing, contributed to what Achebe called the "almost complete disaster for the black races . . . the warped mental attitudes of both black and white . . . the traumatic experience" that was the legacy of Africa's long encounter with Europe. Achebe read Basden's and others' accounts and absorbed them. . . .

The Society of *Things Fall Apart*

Things Fall Apart is "an act of atonement with my past, the ritual return and homage of a prodigal son." Conceived first as a story that would deal with the lives of three men in a family over three generations—Okonkwo, Nwoye (who later takes the Christian name Isaac), and Obi Okonkwo—the novel was originally divided into three parts with two of the parts eventually expanded to tell the full story of only two lives, those of Okonkwo (in *Things Fall Apart*) and Obi Okonkwo (in *No Longer at Ease*). Nwoye's complete story has never been told (though interesting speculative articles on what that life might have comprised have been published by critics and scholars).

Chinua Achebe. AP Images.

Things Fall Apart primarily tells the story of Okonkwo and his life and career in the village of Umuofia. His father is Unoka, a wastrel, known in "all the clan for the weakness of his machete and his hoe" (who nonetheless embodies qualities admirable in themselves if not admired and supported in the clan). Okonkwo is determined through hard work to achieve the highest titles in his clan. He embodies the qualities most valued by his people (if in an exaggerated form)—energy, a strong sense of purpose, and a sense of communal cooperativeness that at the same time is marked by a strong sense of individuality.

When readers meet him, Okonkwo's fame is already established: "Okonkwo was well-known throughout the nine villages and even beyond. His fame rested on solid personal achievements." As a young man he had thrown Amalinze, the Cat, "the great wrestler who for seven years was unbeaten from Umuofia to Mbaino." Okonkwo thus brought "honor to his village." Since that time his fame has grown like a "bush fire in the harmattan": he has achieved wealth and wives and children and is a member of the highest council of the clan. Okonkwo's rise to a position of wealth and authority is in part accounted for by the strength of his will, his back, and his arms. Burdened with an improvident father and—due to one very bad year—an early failure as a farmer, Okonkwo does not yield to despair: "it always surprised him that he did not sink under the load of despair. He knew he had been a fierce fighter, but that year had been enough to break the heart of a lion." Recognizing his capacity for survival, he believes that "'since I survived that year . . . I shall survive anything.' He put it down to his inflexible will." Okonkwo's whole life is "dominated by fear, the fear of failure and weakness . . . and so Okonkwo's whole life was ruled by one passion—to hate everything that his father Unoka had loved."

In metaphysical terms, however, in accordance with the beliefs of the clan, Okonkwo's success is attributed to his *chi*. In the concept of the *chi*, Achebe secures the philosophical basis of the novel and reveals the essential duality of Igbo belief. Okonkwo's success is attributed to a benevolent *chi*. The Ghanaian writer and critic Kofi Awoonor says that "the 'chi' is personal god or man's deital expression, the ultimate mission brought by man from the creator's house, a deity that makes each man's unique personality or being." Relating this to Achebe's achievement, Awoonor writes: "Achebe's thematic construction and dramatisation of the conflict in *Things Fall Apart* utilises the 'chi' concept. The structure of the novel is firmly based in the principles that are derived from this piece of Igbo ontological evidence. Okonkwo's life and actions seem to be prescribed by those immutable laws inherent in the 'chi' concept. It is the one significant principle that determines the rhythm and tragic grandeur of the novel. Okonkwo's rise and fall are seen in the significant way in which he challenges his 'chi' to battle."

Okonkwo's story is set against the background of daily life in Umuofia, an agrarian society governed by rules of religion and politics, always discussed, debated, and amended as circumstances dictate. It is a democratic society in which titles are taken (or given) on merit and can be taken away if the proscriptions for holding them are violated. The tension in the society and, at the same time, its stability arise out of the balance struck between individuality—which in Okonkwo's case displays itself in a single-minded pursuit of acquiring wealth and thus respect and influence—and communality. Individual enterprise is valued and rewarded. But a strong religious principle keeps this individualism in check. Achebe has written that "Igbo society has always been materialistic. This may sound strange because Igbo life had at the same time a strong spiritual dimension—controlled by other gods, ancestors, personal spirits or 'chi' and magic." . . .

The meaning of Achebe's novel is sustained by the consummate control he has over his materials, as these are presented in a manner appropriate to all of the moods and modes of the story. Achebe has said in many places that the words must sound right in his ear before he sets them down. His statement about the kind of English appropriate to the writer's task is well known: "The price a world language must be prepared to pay is submission to many different kinds of use. The African writer should aim to use English in a way that brings out his message best without altering the language to the extent that its value as a medium for international exchange will be lost. He should aim at fashioning out an English which is at once universal and able to carry his peculiar experience."

Things Fall Apart is an account of colonial history from the point of view of the colonized rather than the colonizer: the perspective is African ontology instead of Eurocentric histography. . . .

Contributions to Nigeria and Literature

Achebe [has been] involved in the quest to determine a just system of governance for Nigerians and to ally his thoughts to the place of literature in serving society's needs. In 1986 Achebe was awarded the Nigerian National Merit Award for the second time. In his acceptance speech he acknowledged that "the comprehensive goal of a developing nation like Nigeria is, of course, development or its somewhat better variant, modernization" and that literature is central in the quest for achieving this goal. . . .

Chinua Achebe dominates the African novel and has a central place in contemporary literature because he has reflectively and unobtrusively modified the traditions of fiction, deriving forms distinctively his own for the purpose of envisaging and conveying experiences that are deeply convincing. Profundity, discriminating insight, mental and moral fastidiousness, elegance, and lucidity—these are the hallmarks of Achebe's art.

Chinua Achebe's Philosophy of Fiction

Jerome Brooks, interviewing Chinua Achebe

Jerome Brooks, who died in 2007, was professor emeritus of English at City College of New York.

In this transcript of live interviews with Brooks, Chinua Achebe talks about his initial interest in writing, which began with the stories he heard in his home as a child. In later years, he found that stories about African people, including his people, the Igbo, did not depict their lives and culture accurately. Brooks asks Achebe to describe his efforts at publishing Things Fall Apart, *including the fact that the original manuscript was neglected by the British typing service he entrusted with its production.*

This interview took place on two very different occasions. The first meeting was before a live audience at the Unterberg Poetry Center of the Ninety-second Street Y[MCA in New York City]. . . .

The second session took place on an early fall day at Achebe's house on the beautiful grounds where he lives in upstate New York. . . .

Achebe's Early Interest in Stories

INTERVIEWER

Jerome Brooks: Would you tell us something about the Achebe family and growing up in an Igbo village, your early education, and whether there was anything there that pointed you that early in the direction of writing?

CHINUA ACHEBE: I think the thing that clearly pointed me there was my interest in stories. Not necessarily *writing*

Jerome Brooks, "The Art of Fiction No. 139, Chinua Achebe," *The Paris Review*, vol. 133, Winter 1994, pp. 1–25. Copyright © 1994 by *The Paris Review*. Reprinted with permission of The Wylie Agency LLC.

stories, because at that point, writing stories was not really viable. So you didn't think of it. But I knew I loved stories, stories told in our home, first by my mother, then by my elder sister—such as the story of the tortoise—whatever scraps of stories I could gather from conversations, just from hanging around, sitting around when my father had visitors. When I began going to school, I loved the stories I read. They were different, but I loved them too. My parents were early converts to Christianity in my part of Nigeria. They were not just converts; my father was an evangelist, a religious teacher. He and my mother traveled for thirty-five years to different parts of Igboland, spreading the gospel. I was the fifth of their six children. By the time I was growing up, my father had retired and had returned with his family to his ancestral village.

When I began going to school and learned to read, I encountered stories of other people and other lands. In one of my essays, I remember the kind of things that fascinated me. Weird things, even, about a wizard who lived in Africa and went to China to find a lamp . . . Fascinating to me because they were about things remote, and almost ethereal.

Then I grew older and began to read about adventures in which I didn't know that I was supposed to be on the side of those savages who were encountered by the good white man. I instinctively took sides with the white people. They were fine! They were excellent. They were intelligent. The others were not . . . they were stupid and ugly. That was the way I was introduced to the danger of not having your own stories. There is that great proverb—that until the lions have their own historians, the history of the hunt will always glorify the hunter. That did not come to me until much later. Once I realized that, I had to be a writer. I had to be that historian. It's not one man's job. It's not one person's job. But it is something we have to do, so that the story of the hunt will also reflect the agony, the travail—the bravery, even, of the lions.

Influenced by University Experience

You were among the first graduates of the great University of Ibadan. What was it like in the early years of that university, and what did you study there? Has it stuck with you in your writing?

Ibadan was, in retrospect, a great institution. In a way, it revealed the paradox of the colonial situation, because this university college was founded towards the end of British colonial rule in Nigeria. If they did any good things, Ibadan was one of them. It began as a college of London University, because under the British you don't rush into doing any of those things like universities just like that. You start off as an appendage of somebody else. You go through a period of tutelage. We were the University College of Ibadan of London. So I took a degree from London University. That was the way it was organized in those days. One of the signs of independence, when it came, was for Ibadan to become a full-fledged university.

I began with science, then English, history, and religion. I found these subjects exciting and very useful. Studying religion was new to me and interesting because it wasn't only Christian theology; we also studied West African religions. My teacher there, Dr. Parrinder, now an emeritus professor of London University, was a pioneer in the area. He had done extensive research in West Africa, in Dahomey. For the first time, I was able to see the systems—including my own—compared and placed side by side, which was really exciting. I also encountered a professor, James Welch, in that department, an extraordinary man, who had been chaplain to King George VI, chaplain to the BBC, and all kinds of high-powered things before he came to us. He was a very eloquent preacher. On one occasion, he said to me, We may not be able to teach you what you need or what you want. We can only teach you what we know. I thought that was wonderful. That was really the best education I had. I didn't learn anything there that I really needed, except this kind of attitude. I have had to go out on my own. The English department was a very good example of what I mean. The people there would have laughed at the idea that any of us would become a writer. That didn't really cross their minds. I remember on one occasion a departmental prize was offered. They put up a notice—write a short story over the long vacation for the departmental prize. I'd never written a short story before, but when I got home, I thought, Well, why not. So I wrote one and submitted it. Months passed; then finally one day there was a notice on the board announcing the result. It said that no prize was awarded because no entry was up to the standard. They named me, said that my story deserved mention. Ibadan in those days was not a dance you danced with snuff in one palm. It was a dance you danced with all your body. So when Ibadan said you deserved mention, that was very high praise.

I went to the lecturer who had organized the prize and said, You said my story wasn't really good enough but it was interesting. Now what was wrong with it? She said, Well, it's the form. It's the wrong form. So I said, Ah, can you tell me about this? She said, Yes, but not now. I'm going to play tennis; we'll talk about it. Remind me later, and I'll tell you. This went on for a whole term. Every day when I saw her, I'd say, Can we talk about form? She'd say, No, not now. We'll talk about it later. Then at the very end she saw me and said, You know, I looked at your story again and actually there's nothing wrong with it. So that was it! That was all I learned from the English department about writing short stories. You really have to go out on your own and do it. . . .

The Source of the Title

*The titles of your first two books—*Things Fall Apart *and* No Longer at Ease—*are from modern Irish and American poets. Other black writers—I'm thinking particularly of Paule Mar-*

*shall—borrow from [Irish poet William Butler] Yeats. I wonder
if Yeats and [American-born British poet T.S.] Eliot are among
your favorite poets.*

They are. Actually, I wouldn't make too much of that. I
was showing off more than anything else. As I told you, I took
a general degree, with English as part of it, and you had to
show some evidence of that. But I liked Yeats! That wild Irish-
man. I really loved his love of language, his flow. His chaotic
ideas seemed to me just the right thing for a poet. Passion! He
was always on the right side. He may be wrongheaded, but his
heart was always on the right side. He wrote beautiful poetry.
It had the same kind of magic about it that I mentioned the
wizard had for me. I used to make up lines with anything that
came into my head, anything that sounded interesting. So
Yeats was that kind of person for me. It was only later I dis-
covered his theory of circles or cycles of civilization. I wasn't
thinking of that at all when it came time to find a title. That
phrase "things fall apart" seemed to me just right and appropriate.

T. S. Eliot was quite different. I had to study him at Ibadan.
He had a kind of priestly erudition—eloquence, but of a different kind. Scholarly to a fault. But I think the poem from
which I took the title of *No Longer at Ease*, the one about the
three magi, is one of the great poems in the English language.
These people who went and then came back to their countries
were "no longer at ease" . . . I think that that is great—the use
of simple language, even when things talked about are profound, very moving, very poignant. So that's really all there is
to it. But you'll notice that after those first two titles I didn't
do it anymore.

First Manuscript Nearly Lost

*I once heard your English publisher, Alan Hill, talk about how
you sent the manuscript of* Things Fall Apart *to him.*

That was a long story. The first part of it was how the manuscript was nearly lost. In 1957 I was given a scholarship to go to London and study for some months at the BBC. I had a draft of *Things Fall Apart* with me, so I took it along to finish it. When I got to the BBC, one of my friends—there were two of us from Nigeria—said, Why don't you show this to Mr. Phelps? Gilbert Phelps, one of the instructors of the BBC school, was a novelist. I said, What? No! This went on for some time. Eventually I was pushed to do it and I took the manuscript and handed it to Mr. Phelps. He said, Well . . . all right, the way I would today if anyone brought me a manuscript. He was not really enthusiastic. Why should he be? He took it anyway, very politely. He was the first person, outside of myself, to say, I think this is interesting. In fact, he felt so strongly that one Saturday he was compelled to look for me and tell me. I had traveled out of London; he found out where I was, phoned the hotel, and asked me to call him back. When I was given this message, I was completely floored. I said, Maybe he doesn't like it. But then why would he call me if he doesn't like it? So it must be he *likes* it. Anyway, I was very excited. When I got back to London, he said, This is wonderful. Do you want me to show it to my publishers? I said, Yes, but not yet, because I had decided that the form wasn't right. Attempting to do a saga of three families, I was covering too much ground in this first draft. So I realized that I needed to do something drastic, really give it more body. So I said to Mr. Phelps, OK, I am very grateful but I'd like to take this back to Nigeria and look at it again. Which is what I did.

When I was in England, I had seen advertisements about typing agencies; I had learned that if you really want to make a good impression, you should have your manuscript well typed. So, foolishly, from Nigeria I parceled my manuscript—handwritten, by the way, and the only copy in the whole world—wrapped it up and posted it to this typing agency that advertised in the *Spectator*. They wrote back and said, Thank you for your manuscript. We'll charge thirty-two pounds. That was what they wanted for two copies and which they had to receive before they started. So I sent thirty-two pounds in British postal order to these people and then I heard no more. Weeks passed, and months. I wrote and wrote and wrote. No answer. Not a word. I was getting thinner and thinner and thinner. Finally, I was very lucky. My boss at the broadcasting house was going home to London on leave. A very stubborn Englishwoman. I told her about this. She said, Give me their name and address. When she got to London she went there! She said, What's this nonsense? They must have been shocked, because I think their notion was that a manuscript sent from *Africa*—well, there's really nobody to follow it up. The British don't normally behave like that. It's not done, you see. But something from Africa was treated differently. So when this woman, Mrs. Beattie, turned up in their office and said, What's going on? they were confused. They said, The manuscript was sent but customs returned it. Mrs. Beattie said, Can I see your dispatch book? They had no dispatch book. So she said, Well, send this thing, typed up, back to him in the next week, or otherwise you'll hear about it. So soon after that, I received the typed manuscript of *Things Fall Apart*. One copy, not two. No letter at all to say what happened. My publisher, Alan Hill, rather believed that the thing was simply neglected, left in a corner gathering dust. That's not what happened. These people did not want to return it to me and had no intention of doing so. Anyway, when I got it I sent it back up to Heinemann. They had never seen an African novel. They didn't know what to do with it. Someone told them, Oh, there's a professor of economics at London School of Economics and Political Science who just came back from those places. He might be able to advise you. Fortunately, Don Macrae was a very literate professor, a wonderful man. I got to know him later. He wrote what they said was the shortest report they ever had on any novel—seven words: "The best first novel since the war." So that's how I got launched.

A Small Beginning

Heinemann was also perplexed as to how many copies should be printed...

Oh yes. They printed very, very few. It was a risk. Not something they'd ever done before. They had no idea if anybody would want to read it. It went out of print very quickly. It would have stayed that way if Alan Hill hadn't decided that he was going to gamble even more and launch a paperback edition of this book. Other publishers thought it was mad, that this was crazy. But that was how the African Writers Series came in to existence. In the end, Alan Hill was made a Commander of the British Empire for bringing into existence a body of literature they said was among the biggest developments in British literature of [the twentieth] century. So it was a very small beginning, but it caught fire.

Achebe Feels a Special Commitment as an African Writer

Romanus Okey Muoneke

Romanus Okey Muoneke is a member of the English Department at the University of St. Thomas in Houston, Texas. He earned a BA from the University of Nigeria and a PhD in English from the University of Houston. He has taught in Nigeria, Ireland, and the United States.

Muoneke states in the following selection that in Africa, art and society are inseparable. African writers, such as Chinua Achebe, feel a commitment to the community to portray its experience truthfully, a greater responsibility than is felt by European artists. Further, Achebe believes he has a duty to influence African society and politics by educating its people about the dignity and value of their own culture. Muoneke quotes Achebe as insisting that an African writer who avoids addressing the major issues confronting present-day Africa will be irrelevant.

In his essays and interviews Achebe ranges widely over a number of vital issues. One of his preferred subjects is the role of the creative writer in society. His theory on the writer's role and commitment can be summed up under the following propositions:

(a) Art, including literature, is a communal celebration in Africa.

(b) The African writer cannot but be committed, for there is no room for art for art's sake, given the African situation.

Romanus Okey Muoneke, "Chapter One: The Artist and Society," in *Art, Rebellion and Redemption: A Reading of the Novels of the Chinua Achebe*, New York, NY: Peter Lang, 1994, pp. 11–36. Copyright © 1994 Peter Lang Publishing, Inc., New York. All rights reserved. Reproduced by permission.

(c) Writers, as individuals exceptionally gifted, carry with them social responsibilities, among which is rendering vision and a sense of order to a non-perfect society.

(d) The special role of the writer is to teach.

Art and Society Are One

Achebe's theory of art is rounded on the African belief in the indivisibility of art and society. The *mbari* ceremony found among the Owerri Igbo of Nigeria has been constantly used by Achebe as a point of departure to show that art functions as a communal celebration of life. As Achebe explains in "African Literature as Celebration," celebration does not simply mean a remembrance of blessings and happy events, it includes other experiences: "all significant encounters which man makes in his journey through life, especially new, unaccustomed and thus potentially threatening encounters."

The *mbari* example demands a total involvement of the participating artists who work in holy seclusion with selected members of the community to produce art works that reflect the life of the entire community in its diversity—gods, men, women, animals, historic events (the coming of the white man, for example), the village scandal, etc.—all are represented in the final ensemble. . . . African art, as represented in the *mbari* culture, is therefore not an individual affair but a "creative communal enterprise" in which the community functions both as the "beneficiary" and the "active partaker" of the experience. . . .

Story Has Power to Transform

The theory of the story as a vehicle for transforming the human consciousness is important in understanding Achebe's literary vocation. The story is for him an indispensable medium for cultivating virtue and ideal values. It is not mere entertainment, nor simply a mode of conveying experience, but more functionally, a means to redeem the human system, to give it a soul, to transform it.

Since the cosmology [structure of the universe] of the Igbo is based on tradition that is fluid rather than fixed, "anyone seeking an insight into their world must seek it along their own way," among which paths is the medium of the folktale. . . .

A difference exists between European writers and their African counterparts. In Achebe's observation, it is marked by the way they relate to their communities. In "The Novelist as Teacher" he writes, "We have learned from Europe that a writer or an artist lives on the fringe of society—wearing a beard and a peculiar dress and generally behaving in a strange, unpredictable way. He is in revolt against society, which in turn looks on him with suspicion if not hostility." The European writer is not accountable to the community, the African is. Again, European art "exists independently of us, of all mankind," whereas the African art exists "to serve a down-to-earth necessity," "to minister to a basic human need" in society. Achebe continues in "Africa and Her Writers":

> Our ancestors created their myths and legends and told their stories for a human purpose . . . they made their sculptures in wood and terra cotta, stone and bronze to serve the needs of their times. Their artists lived and moved and had their being in society and created their works for the good of that society.

African Writers Must Be Committed

Achebe is here concerned with one aspect of the European view on art for art's sake which has left its imprint on the contemporary European literary scene. The comparison with the European attitude only serves to underscore one point, that art and society are inseparable in Africa, past and present, which explains why African writers must devote their creative energy to the service of society.

Achebe further argues that art for art's sake has no place in the African world. He once began a lecture on this tone of denunciation: "*Art for art's sake is just another piece of deodorized dog shit.*" He has since tried to modify this-extreme position. He now acknowledges the importance of individual talent and artistic eloquence, but he feels that the importance of such gifts is highlighted by a recognition of the "seminal potentialities of the community." He now explains how and why the European art and literature should experience a phase of despair and thus be preoccupied with the "sickness of the human condition": Europe may have "overreached [herself] in technical achievement without spiritual growth." Achebe insists that, given the African situation, aloofness and escapism should have no place in the African writer. He must be committed.

On the writer's commitment, Achebe's stand is unflinching. In "The African Writer and the Biafran Cause" he states:

> It is clear to me that an African creative writer who tries to avoid the big social and political issues of contemporary Africa will end up being completely irrelevant—like that absurd man in the proverb who leaves his burning house to pursue a rat fleeing from the flames.

Achebe made this statement when the Nigerian civil war was raging. He had identified fully with the Biafran cause, functioning as the Biafran P.R.O. abroad. [Biafra is a state of Nigeria inhabited mainly by the Igbo that existed as a secessionist state for several years.] . . .

Achebe's Definition of Commitment

Achebe defined commitment as "the sense of social obligation or strong attachment to a cause, and the use of art, in this case literature, to define that obligation and advance the cause." His own writings are an application of this concept, which all the more makes him a committed writer. His major works relate to the history of his people, in which their problems, successes and failures are addressed. *Things Fall Apart,* his first novel, examines the Igbo society prior to and at the

Richard von Weizsaecker (left), former German president, congratulates Nigerian author Chinua Achebe after Achebe is awarded the prestigious Peace Prize of the German publishing industry in 2002 in Frankfurt. © Frank May/dpa/epa/Corbis.

point of confrontation with colonial rule. *Arrow of God* shows the same society as it tries to accommodate the new system. These two novels are devoted to the past, a past that had its

glories as well as its disappointments, a past in need of definition because of the distortions by which the colonialists had
portrayed it. *No Longer at Ease* examines life in Nigeria at the
threshold of independence when the noble values of the past
suffered terrible recidivism as two cultures met and engaged
war in the protagonist, Obi Okonkwo. *A Man of the People*
turns the light on the politicians of post-independence Nigeria. They are found wanting in many ways and are seen to be
incapable of giving the people the right leadership. A military
intervention ends the novel—an event that coincidentally took
place in Nigeria nine days after the novel was published.
Achebe's most recent novel, *Anthills of the Savannah* focuses
on the country under the military. He alerts the reader to the
cultural, social, and political life of a fictitious West African
country which is no other than Nigeria. *Girls at War*, a collection of his short stories, and *Beware Soul Brother* (poems) are
set in the Nigerian civil war. In Achebe's novels, society is fully
alive; it moves and breathes. Many Africans who read Achebe's
novels easily identify with the characters and events as is evident from the numerous letters the author received after the
publication of *Things Fall Apart*. In his essay, "The Uses of African Literature," Achebe writes, "A writer who feels a strong
and abiding concern for his fellows cannot evade the role of
social critic which is the contemporary expression of commitment to the community." This commitment, he maintains, has
always been at the essence of African literature. It is no wonder that practically all his works are concerned with the affairs
of his community.

Achebe may not have used the word redemption to describe the role the writer plays in society, yet his position,
when closely examined, comes to this, that the writer's duty is
to change society for the better. . . .

The redemptive role of the writer introduces a note of optimism in a world that is made more complex by what Achebe

calls the "powers of event" (that is, that which we cannot control—accident or chance) and man's wrong deeds. . . .

The Writer as Teacher

Like God the Creator who created order out of chaos and saw that his work was "good," the writer, according to Achebe, renders vision and order to our chaotic world. It is the special office of the writer to "recreate the world for the advantage of humanity," a task which also involves creating the "new man," that is, a society guided by solid moral principles, for as Achebe attests in a presentation he made with [black American writer James] Baldwin, African art is morally based. Hence, the writer does not concern himself with mere aesthetics; he has to provide society with "something solid and permanent," external values that will underlie the moral consciousness of the "new man." With African societies caught at the crossroads of cultures as a result of colonialism, the modern African writer would have to retrieve from the past worthy ancestral values and attitudes—respect for age, for parents, emphasis on the family, etc.—which are capable of redeeming an already confused society.

The writer is a teacher, and African writers feel they have a special mission to change their society by the process of education. Achebe will be remembered by generations for his new emphasis on the educational role of the writer. Certainly, he is not the first to expound the concept; [Torquato] Tasso, [Philip] Sidney, [Thomas] Carlyle, [Robert] Lowell, [Jean-Paul] Sartre, all mentioned it in their works. [William] Wordsworth was known to have said, "Every great Poet is a Teacher; I wish either to be considered as a Teacher, or as nothing." Wordsworth taught his audience that the common man is a worthy subject for poetry. Achebe also regards himself as a teacher, but what is even more important is the prominence he has given this role in the African world. . . .

Writers Should Teach Pride

The most important lesson African writers need to teach their people is self-esteem. They must teach them "that their past—with all its imperfections—was not one long night of savagery from which the first Europeans acting on God's behalf delivered them." The aim of writing *Things Fall Apart* and *Arrow of God* could not be more explicit. In these two novels, in particular, Achebe makes the strong case that the Igbo culture and institutions possessed beauty and substance. Igbo life and society were not the grotesque creations that the colonialists had made them out to be. Furthermore, the image of the African has suffered terribly in the hands of European colonizers and writers, and it is the duty of the writer, "a human being with heightened sensitivities" to correct this distorted image and "restore to his people a good opinion of themselves." In the same essay Achebe writes:

> Whether we like to face up to it or not, Africa has been the most insulted continent in the world. Africans' very claim to humanity has been questioned at various times, their persons abused, their intelligence insulted. These things have happened in the past and have gone on happening today. We [writers] have a duty to bring them to an end for our own sakes, for the sake of our children, and indeed for the safety and happiness of the world.

The irony of the situation is that even the victims of the colonial denigration ultimately came to accept colonial life-style with awe and admiration, and to perceive everything African "as something to be ashamed of and snapped at the earliest opportunity." As a writer whose duty is to teach and correct, Achebe reacts thus in "The Novelist as Teacher":

> Here then is an adequate revolution for me to espouse—to help my society regain belief in itself and put away the complexes of the years of denigration and self-abasement. And it

is essentially a question of education, in the best sense of the word. Here I think my aims and the deepest aspirations of my society meet.

Achebe carefully selects his words in this quotation. It is a question of education and, although not directly mentioned but implied, teaching.

The significance of "teacher" to the African is worth mentioning. The one who teaches provides knowledge and insight to the taught. In African communities, especially in the 50's and 60's, teachers were highly revered not only because of the knowledge and insight they provided but also because they were looked upon as a individuals of dignity and authority, and as social ambassadors or representatives of society. Like the ancient Jewish priest who knew the Jewish law and ritual and had authority to interpret them, the teacher in Africa was expected to be knowledgeable about the society, including its norms and values. The relationship between teachers and their community was often based on love and trust. When Achebe chooses to use the word "teacher" to explain the role of the writer, he is well aware of the strong connotations the word carries.

Toward the end of "The Novelist as Teacher" Achebe makes it clear that the writer's role does not end with teaching Africans about their moral goodness and the nature of creation, teaching them that "there is nothing disgraceful about the African weather, that the palm tree is a fit subject of poetry," there needs to be "re-education and regeneration."

Social Issues in Literature

CHAPTER 2

Things Fall Apart and Colonialism

Okonkwo's Actions Foreshadow Colonialism's Impact on Traditional Values

Christopher Heywood

A graduate of Oxford University, Christopher Heywood developed a special commitment to African/South African literature when he served as head of the English Department at the University of Ife, Nigeria, while on leave from England's Sheffield University, where he was a member of the faculty from 1956 to 1988. Heywood has since published or edited numerous literary reviews and books on African and South African literature.

In this selection, Heywood notes that Okonkwo's violent actions set him on a course of alienation from the traditions of his Igbo culture and from the earth goddess. His inclination for rash action and masculine assertiveness are an overreaction to his father's weakness. Okonkwo's ultimate destruction is symbolic of the destruction of his community's way of life as the colonial authority asserts itself and its culture.

The story of Okonkwo unfolds around five actions of violence and desecration. Each action calls for expiation [atonement] rather than judgement, for the restoration of social order, and each has tragic implications for the community. Nine villages, Abame, Aninta, Ezimili, Ire, Mbaino, Umuero, Umunso, Umuochi, and Umuofia, constitute the community of 'Umuofia' to which Okonkwo is born. The social panorama, like the chain of tragic events, unfolds as it would to a child of Umuofia, and each stage of Okonkwo's destiny represents a moment of transition into a wider world.

Christopher Heywood, "The Characters in the Story," in *Chinua Achebe: "Things Fall Apart"—A Critical View*, edited by Yolande Cantu, The British Council, 1985, pp. 8–13.

With each phase of the story, Okonkwo moves in a widening circle, starting in the household, moving outwards to the village in its relationship with Mbaino, then onwards into the neighbouring territories of Mbanta and other surrounding Igbo communities. In the final phase of the action, Okonkwo comes into conflict with the international setting of colonial conflict, and lastly in committing suicide by hanging himself, he becomes an abomination to the earth itself. His friend Obierika explains to the District Commissioner, whose heavy-handed intervention has precipitated the suicide:

> 'We cannot bury him. Only strangers can. We shall pay your men to do it. When he has been buried we will then do our duty by him. We shall make sacrifices to cleanse the desecrated land.'

From the outset the violent actions of Okonkwo are seen as offences against Ani, goddess of the earth, rather than as actions which are wrong only in their being hurtful to other members of society. The earth and its products are the guarantees of survival and all actions are referred to its central mysteries. Thus, there are two incidents of wife-beating which signal the violent nature of the hero in the opening chapters. But it is the one which offends the goddess of earth, when Okonkwo beats his third wife, Ojiugo, during the Week of Peace which is dedicated to prosperity, peace and farm work, that attracts the rebuke of Ezěani, priest of the cult of Ani. A grave warning is sounded by Okonkwo's closest friend, Obierika, whose voice speaks many of the traditional strengths of the society, when Okonkwo kills the boy Ikemefuna.

Both these offences are contained within the village community, but the third brings a harsh retribution in the form of exile for the hero and his family to Mbanta, the neighbouring territory of his mother. At the funeral rites of Ezeudu, an elder of Umuofia, Okonkwo's gun accidentally explodes and a stray fragment kills Ezeudu's sixteen-year-old son. This is a 'female crime', since it was not intended. Thus the seven years of exile prepare the hero for the final challenge when he returns to his community. On his return, Okonkwo finds Umuofia under the authority of a white District Commissioner and black officers, teachers and Christian converts who repudiate or do not understand the traditions of Umuofia. Obierika here explains the process which gives the book its title: 'The white man ... has put a knife on the things that held us together and we have fallen apart'.

Okonkwo's last actions are deliberate, impulsive, and final. Suicide, the concluding act of desecration, is the only alternative to capture and execution, which would await him if he were brought to trial for having cut off the head of a messenger who had been sent to quell a meeting of protest in Umuofia. The events leading to this catastrophe are swift and inevitable. The arrival of a second missionary, Mr Smith, who differs from his predecessor, Mr Brown, in his severity towards the Igbo religion and favouritism towards over-zealous converts to the new religion, precipitates a crisis. Enoch, a bigoted convert, unmasks and thus desecrates one of the *egwugwu* masqueraders. In protest, the *egwugwu* group burn to the ground first Enoch's house, and next the church. Okonkwo and his five companions, who are summoned by the District Commissioner, are tricked into becoming hostages until a fine is paid. The cruel treatment they receive in the cells, and other grievances among the Umuofians, lead to a protest meeting. When five court messengers arrive to report that the District Commissioner wishes the meeting to cease, Okonkwo instantly decapitates the leading messenger; suicide, his last action, is the only way ahead for him.

The events of the tragic story are inextricably interwoven with the religious and historical themes which form the basis of the novel. At all points in his destiny, Okonkwo is shown to be inseparable from the beliefs of his community. Achebe places his hero in a clearly marked pattern of family, household and friendship relationships. Unoka, Okonkwo's father, is a weak man who prefers music, pleasure and debt to social responsibility. As a result, Okonkwo overcompensates and commits himself to a life of exaggerated masculine valour, self-aggrandizement and prominence. He despises women and is 'ruled by one passion—to hate everything that his father Unoka had loved'. This estrangement is in itself a betrayal of African family tradition. It leads in its turn to an estrangement between Okonkwo and his eldest son, Nwoye. In adopting the newly arrived Christian faith, Nwoye repudiates his father's cult of self-assertion and reverts to the immersion in sensuous enjoyment which his grandfather had represented. Christianity appeals to him for literary and musical reasons: 'the poetry of the new religion, something felt in the marrow', and 'a relief within as the hymn poured into his parched soul' are the causes of his conversion. Nwoye's conversion represents the completion of a cycle of action across three generations.

Okonkwo's alienation from the best traditions of his inherited culture is dramatically illustrated in the circumstances surrounding the death of Ikemefuna. This boy had been bequeathed to him as a hostage following his successful conduct of reprisals against the neighbouring village of Mbaino, where an Umuofian had been killed. The Oracle foretells the death of the boy and thus his killing does not call for expiation; rather, the two days' revulsion of feeling which overtakes Okonkwo is a natural retribution for the act of violence. For their part, the community interprets this prophecy half-heartedly. When the appointed day arrives, the elders strike a feeble blow which misses the boy, hitting instead the pot which he is carrying. Ikemefuna lives still, but in running to his adopted father, Okonkwo, he runs to his death. Okonkwo, as much a literal interpreter of prophecy as the vengeful missionary Smith in the final action, had insisted on accompanying the sacrificial expedition to the forest despite the earnest entreaty to the contrary of Ogbuefi Ezeudu, the oldest man in the village whose son he later kills through carelessness. 'I want you to have nothing to do with it. He calls you his father', Ogbuefi Ezeudu urges. But Okonkwo is resolute. At the last instant, when Ikemefuna runs to him for protection, Okonkwo is undermined for a second time by his rash repudiation of his father's characteristic irresolution: 'he was afraid to be thought weak' and he strikes the fatal blow with his own hand. Obierika is uncompromising in his informal condemnation of this action: 'What you have done will not please the Earth. It is the kind of action for which the goddess wipes out whole families'. Foreshadowing his own extinction in the final action, Okonkwo pleads: 'The Earth cannot punish me for obeying her messenger', but Obierika diplomatically demurs: 'That is true . . . But if the Oracle said that my son should be killed I would neither dispute it nor be the one to do it'.

Thus, in a complex narrative, Achebe develops his main characters through a series of actions in successive phases and widening relationships, and never loses sight of the underlying values of African society and family life.

Okonkwo's Loss of Identity Parallels the Experience of Colonized Africans

Ifeoma Onyemelukwe

Ifeoma Onyemelukwe is a teacher in the Department of French, in the Faculty of Arts, at Ahmadu Bello University, the largest university in Nigeria. Her literary reviews have appeared in journals such as Neohelicon, *which publishes studies in comparative and world literature.*

In the following selection, Onyemelukwe explains that Okonkwo's identity stems from his prowess and fame as a wrestler, warrior, and farmer, qualities that distinguish him in the Igbo culture. He loses his stature and identity as a result of a rash act. Upon his return to his village after a seven-year absence, Okonkwo's attempt to regain his identity is unsuccessful and ends in his suicide. Onyemelukwe proposes that Okonkwo's tragedy parallels the loss of identity and dignity of the Igbo and many other African peoples during the colonial era.

Identity crisis . . . has implication for the personality the individual turns out to be as a young adult and also for coping with problems of adolescents and youth in the micro-society (family) as well as the macro-society. The ideas the individual has about himself, his family, friends and society in adolescence tend to influence his self-concept and shape his identity. A time comes when he decides amidst the various perceptions of him that "This is what I want to be." His identity crisis is resolved and he comes up with his own identity. In other words his identity is formed. . . .

Ifeoma Onyemelukwe, "Search for Lost Identity in Achebe's *Things Fall Apart*," in *Emerging Perspectives on Chinua Achebe; vol. 1, Omenka: The Master Artist*, edited by Ernest N. Emenyonu, Trenton, NJ: Africa World Press, Inc., 2004, pp. 35–47. Copyright © 2004 Ernest N. Emenyonu. All rights reserved. Reproduced by permission.

The pertinent question is: Does the Igbo culture help in shaping Okonkwo's identity and personality? . . .

Roots of Okonkwo's Identity

> Okonkwo was well known throughout the nine villages and even beyond. His fame rested on *solid personal achievements.* As a young man of eighteen he had brought honour to his village by throwing the Cat. Amalinze was the great wrestler who for seven years was unbeaten . . . He was called the Cat . . . It was this man that Okonkwo threw in a fight which . . . was one of the fiercest . . . (emphasis added).

This passage draws the reader's attention to the character, Okonkwo, who has succeeded in having his identity formed. Who is Okonkwo? or What is Okonkwo? Okonkwo, as can be deduced from the cited passage, is the man who was able to resolve his identity crisis in late adolescence. At age 18 he had developed self-confidence, a high self-concept, self-esteem and had high achievement motivation as typical of the average Igbo man. The consequence of this is his reverberating achievement and celebrity. "Okonkwo was well known throughout the nine villages and even beyond." The narrator adds: "His fame had grown like a bush-fire in the harmattan." This figure of speech shows the great wrestler, warrior and farmer to have attained a pedestal where he is enjoying more and more successes.

It should be noted that the Okonkwo being x-rayed in this passage has grown. He is about thirty-eight years old; and grows even the more in the novel. He is now a mature adult member of a male hegemonious [dominate] society which upholds cultural practices that predispose the woman to sub-jugation and oppression and stifle her development and progress in society. . . . He is married to three wives and has many children; polygamy and large unit being also indices of greatness in this culture. *Things Fall Apart* [TFA] depicts very successfully Okonkwo as showing no empathy or sympathy to less fortunate men like his father, Unoka. Such individuals, to his mind, are simply *agbala* (Igbo word for woman) or she-men.

It is not surprising that Okonkwo stands out in the novel as a macho man with a great deal of self-esteem and self-confidence.

The cap fits Okonkwo in many instances in the given description. True, TFA portrays him as one who is neither patient nor tolerant. . . .

Okonkwo is shown in TFA to be an excellent warrior, wrestler and farmer. Where others may have failed, he succeeds. Take, for example, [that] he throws Amalinze, the *Cat* who nobody could defeat in a fight for seven good years. Further, he excels as a farmer, starting with share-cropping, a thing many youths of his time cannot cope with. The third person narrator of TFA has rightly noted that he, Okonkwo, "was clearly cut out for great things."

Essentially, Okonkwo worked hard to attain that great height in society. "His fame rested on solid personal achievements." It was at the age of eighteen that he threw Amalinze, The Cat. In the words of the narrator:

> He (Okonkwo) was still young but he had won fame as the *greatest wrestler* in the nine villages. He was *a wealthy farmer* and had two barns full of yams and *had just married his third wife*. To crown it all, he had taken two titles and had shown *incredible prowess in two inter-tribal wars*; (emphasis mine).

This passage, without doubt, arms the reader with a catalogue of Okonkwo's marks of greatness. The passage, further, throws into relief the fact that he started climbing the ladder of greatness even as a teenager. That, of course, was incumbent on his successful resolution of his identity crisis and subsequent formation of his identity.

That Okonkwo had a serious identity crisis is patent in TFA; what with a father who is slothful, frivolous, given to drinking and merriment, improvident and poor. This lily-livered father who can hardly provide for his family fills Okonkwo with disdain.

Okonkwo's Identity Crisis

Crises and conflict set in. Okonkwo's identity crisis emanates probably from internal contradictions. What he would want to be is at variance with what his father is. The narrator tells us that "even as a little boy" Okonkwo "had resented his father's failure and weakness" and had suffered from people making a mockery of his father, who owes shamelessly and dies without taking even a title. In Igbo culture a man without title is regarded as a woman and treated so. One can imagine Okonkwo's inferiority complex as a child and the shame he had had to put up with. Cognizant of the fact that unlike most of his peers he inherited nothing from his "loafer" of a father he realizes that he has got to work extra hard to make it in life. And he desires to be a success, not a failure like his father. Okonkwo ends up being the polar opposite of his father, Unoka. The choice is his. He rejects the father's image and settles for who he wants to be: The exact opposite of Unoka. He becomes intrinsically motivated, his resentment for his *agbala* of a father being the propelling force. Diligent, determined, dedicated with a sense of direction, Okonkwo becomes famous through 'solid personal achievements.' Okonkwo finally resolves his identity crisis fairly well, evolves his personal identity and emerges as one of the most outstanding achievers of his time in Umuofia and its environs.

That notwithstanding, the author of TFA draws the reader's attention to the adverse impact of identity crisis on Okonkwo's personality development. Okonkwo is transformed into a monomaniac of male dominance. He develops a split personality: the fearless warrior who has brought home human skulls, is dominated by fear, "fear of failure and of weakness," fear of taking after his father. This psychological phobia leads him to hate everything that his father, Unoka, had loved," such as gentleness and idleness. If Okonkwo treats his wives and children tyrannically like Medza's father in Beti's *Mission Terminée*, it is linked to this psychological phobia. The same explanation goes for his inclination to wife-battery and other excesses of his in the novel, like killing Ikemefuna who called him "father" or firing a shot at Ekwefi, his beloved second wife. [Eustace] Palmer puts it succinctly: "this fear which dominates all his actions contributes to his subsequent catastrophe." . . .

Okonkwo Loses His Identity

> His (Okonkwo's) life had been ruled by a great passion to become one of the lords of the clan. That had been his life-spring. And he had all but achieved it. Then everything had been broken. He had been cast out of his clan like a fish on a dry sandy beach, panting. Clearly his personal god or *chi* was not made for great things. A man could not rise beyond the destiny of his *chi*. . . . Here was a man whose *chi* said nay despite his affirmation.

The last sentence is quite paradoxical. The same Okonkwo portrayed in the first part of the novel as saying "yes" and his personal god agreeing is now portrayed as saying "yes" and his *chi* saying 'no'. The Igbo proverb *"Onye kwe chi ya ekwe"* (When a man says 'yes' his *chi* says 'yes' also) is thus depicted with a measure of relativity. In other words, it holds true sometimes while at other times it does not. The second part of TFA describes Okonkwo's tragedy and great fall from grace to grass. During Ezeudu's funeral, Okonkwo inadvertently kills a clansman, one of Ezeudu's sons. This fratricide, because it is accidental, is treated as a female crime (that is, female *ochu*) and attracts for the culprit compulsory banishment for seven years as well as destruction of his house and all his property by way of cleansing or purging the land which has been polluted with the blood of a clansman. Okonkwo thus goes on self-exile to Mbanta, his mother's village, with his wives and children; taking along some of his valuable belongings. At dawn, his compound is besieged by a large crowd of men from Ezeudu's quarters who set his house on fire, destroy his red walls, kill his animals and erase his barn. How are the mighty fallen! Overnight, great Okonkwo, the great warrior, the great farmer, the great wrestler, one of the most outstanding achievers of his time, most respected and revered, loses all he has laboured to achieve just in the twinkle of an eye. His hope of remaining "one of the lords of the clan," is shattered.

His flight to Mbanta implies starting life afresh, from the scratch. It means loss of self-esteem, peace, happiness. His ego is obviously punctured. His fame transforms into shame. His identity crumbles. Crises and conflict set in again. Okonkwo's tragic fall seems to attract the author's sympathy as expressed through the mouth of Okonkwo's intimate friend, Obierika, who though he joins in exacting punishment on Okonkwo, mourns the latter's calamity. . . .

Okonkwo Does Not Regain His Identity

The last third of *Things Fall Apart* offers the reader a glimpse of the frantic efforts made by Okonkwo to regain his lost identity. He is determined to return to Umuofia in a big way and restore all that is lost in a tremendous way. The narrator states that, "even in his first year in exile he had begun to plan for his return." His restoration plan includes: rebuilding his compound on a more magnificent scale, building a bigger barn, marrying two more wives and building huts for them, initiating his sons into the *Ozo* society, a thing done only by men who are really great in the clan; and taking the highest title in the land following his eventual position as the highly esteemed. . . .

In spite of these laudable plans, Okonkwo's return to Umuofia is not memorable. Umuofia does not "appear to have taken any special notice of the warrior's return." This is partly because the clan had undergone profound changes during his period of exile. Moreover, with colonial incursion, missionary activities (establishment of schools and churches and the missionary's proselytism of the natives of Umuofia and its environs), the town of Umuofia is turned into what Okonkwo perceives as "female town". He mourns also for the warlike Umuofia men who have become, to his mind, soft as women. Umuofia, which prior to colonial presence is described as the town of warlike men, now ranks, in Okonkwo's eye, with Abame and Aninta (where titled men climb trees and pound *foofoo* [a staple food of pounded yams] for their wives) and Mbanta, as women's towns. Okonkwo, the central character of TFA, who is manhood personified, cannot stand this drastic change.

Okonkwo incites his clansmen to collective revolt and violence involving the destruction of the church, short of killing Rev. James Smith, the missionary who believes in clear-cut positions, unlike his predecessor, Mr. Brown, whose policy was that of accommodation and compromise with the natives. At the end of the collective action Okonkwo and five others are arrested and hurled into detention where they are beaten and molested, starved, but released on payment of a fine of 250 bags of cowries. This is another thwarted attempt to regain his lost identity.

Okonkwo spoils for vengeance; for a war to fight the white-man and his cohorts. He has reminiscences of his past military conquests in those inter-tribal wars. But can he or his clan contend with the colonizers' naked power? Okika has hardly started his oration, a sensitization campaign to call Umuofians to action to stop colonial incursion, when the gathering was ordered by the head messenger to bring the meeting to a stop. Four other messengers came along with him. Okonkwo cuts off the head messenger's head. There is chaos, and the crowd, with minimal cohesion, disintegrates, leaving Okonkwo isolated. "Why did he do it?" he heard voices asking. Okonkwo, thus defeated, hangs himself behind his compound. What a tragic end! The tragic hero's drama is embedded in the incisive remark of Obierika to the District Commissioner:

> That man (Okonkwo) was one of the greatest men in Umuofia. You drove him to kill himself; and now he will be buried like a dog.

True, Okonkwo will be buried like a dog because for *Ndigbo* [Igbos], suicide is an abomination and one who commits suicide is not fit to be buried by his clansmen but only by strangers.

Is Obierika correct to impute Okonkwo's tragic end to the colonizers? Is his comment endorsed by Achebe? It would seem that the author of TFA shares Obierika's view, judging from the determinant "unnecessarily" that follows the messenger's 'Shut up!' The author-narrator implies that it was pointless trying to silence Obierika given perhaps, that his comment, an oblique attack on the ills of colonialism, makes a lot of sense. Achebe, in this sense, sympathizes with Okonkwo. Does this mean that Achebe is against change in society? Is he conservative? Probably not. As a creative artist, he seems to depict the social reality of the time: collapse of an old order as a result of an invasion by a dominating alien system. There is no denying the fact that Achebe is condemning the negative effects of colonialism, for example, compounding the hero's psychological phobia, fear of failure and weakness, of not being in control of the situation, of having his clansmen turned into a bunch of women, of losing the position where he is seen to dominate all others. It is this accelerated fear that drives him to kill the Head Court Messenger and commit suicide. Achebe, the starry-eyed critic condemns in TFA his people's obnoxious cultural practices which militate against development and progress of man in society, for example, killing of twins, superstitious beliefs, wife-battery, male dominance, women subjugation and oppression. This shows Achebe as a progressive and a reformer.

We feel that Okonkwo is partially responsible for his tragic end. Certain psychological character traits of his, impulsiveness, extreme extroversion, lead him to some of his excesses apart from the fear of being perceived as weak. Furthermore, Okonkwo's tragic fall from grace to grass finds partial explanation in his ruthless resistance to change; an act that is clearly dissonant with the natural inclination of *Ndigbo.*

[Ijeoma] Njaka notes that the evidences of Igbo receptivity to change abound in Igbo folk stories, plays, novels, proverbs and dances. The convenient marriage of the Igbo traditional culture to change has been said to be a source of strength to *Ndigbo* because they are ready for change and maneuverability. *Ndigbo* are essentially tolerant and accommodating. These attributes make them easily receptive to change (e.g. their polyglotism [many languages]), which is one of their methods of regional and global integration. . . .

The same Okonkwo who is compelled to lose his identity in the interest of social cohesion fails to elicit the cooperation of his clansmen when he tries to restore his identity and group identity by cutting colonial authorities to size, which he considers a heroic act. Sadly enough, Okonkwo's move meets with a shattered hope of group solidarity and social cohesion which he enjoyed at the point he was resolving his identity crisis what with those inter-tribal wars/inter-clanic wrestling contests which created opportunities for individual and collective exploits/achievements/successes. This is so because at the point in question, things have greatly fallen apart at both individual and collective levels.

Mirrored Fates

The unraveling of the plot of TFA appears to be pessimistic. Since Okonkwo, the symbol *par excellence* of the Igbo man dies in an attempt to recover his lost identity, does it imply that the attempt by *Ndigbo* to recover their lost identity is more or less suicidal? The Igbo man lost his hard earned identity at the end of the Nigerian Civil War (1970), a war that lasted for 3 years (1967–1970) and decimated badly the population of *Ndigbo*. Completely disarmed, dislocated, destabilized, depersonalized, dehumanized, shunned, abandoned, relegated, excluded, frozen out like banished Okonkwo after committing a fratricide, the Igbo man starts life afresh, from the scratch at the end of the war when every adult Igbo person, no matter how fat his monetary asset is made to receive only £20 (Twenty pounds sterling) in exchange. He has ever since then been making frantic efforts to restore his lost identity and esteem. As Achebe opines:

> The worst thing that can happen to any people is the loss of their dignity and self-respect.

He adds that:

> The writer's duty is to help them regain it by showing them in human terms what happened to them, what they lost ... the novelist's duty is ... to explore in depth the human condition.

In so doing, Achebe is, characteristically, playing out the role of the African writer, which to his mind is that of a teacher.

It is important to remark that Okonkwo's tragedy somewhat transcends that of *Ndigbo* to represent also that of colonized Africans and even subjugated Blacks elsewhere. Achebe appears to say in TFA that many African peoples had lost their dignity in the colonial era just like Okonkwo and they must try to regain it. Specifically, *Ndigbo* lost their identity, and are desperately searching for it to regain it. Thus, the crucial issue in TFA is not just as Achebe puts it "a spiritual search for one's roots," but a frantic search to regain one's lost identity. The latter, of course, subsumes the former.

Language Conveys Male Africans' and Colonists' Power

Ada Uzoamaka Azodo

Ada Uzoamaka Azodo is an adjunct faculty member in the Department of Minority Studies at Indiana University Northwest in Gary, Indiana. She has edited a number of books on women's roles in African literature, including Gender and Sexuality in African Literature and Film.

In the following selection, Azodo explains that the Umuofia community of Things Fall Apart *is one of patriarchal traditions that sustain male superiority. Azodo suggests that the Igbo men use language as a tool to establish power over others. The colonial British administrators, all men, also use language to establish their dominance over the Igbo men. The modes of using power through language in various ways—including proverbs, sarcasm, oratory, voice and status—to achieve various ends are demonstrated in four dialogues Azodo has selected from the novel.*

We shall adopt the investigative method for the study of four selected dialogues in Chinua Achebe's *Things Fall Apart*, in order to gain insights into how male hegemonic [dominance] cults achieve, construct and prolong patriarchal traditions that ensure male superiority. In the Umuofia community of *Things Fall Apart*, Igbo men are constrained to achieve and flaunt it, in order to be seen and respected. To be able to draw upon divergent types of power, men apply different resources during discussions, including the use of irony, riddles, proverbs, sarcasm, jokes, oratory, voice and status, to

Ada Uzoamaka Azodo, "Masculinity, Power and Language in Chinua Achebe's *Things Fall Apart*," in *Emerging Perspectives on Chinua Achebe; vol. 1, Omenka: The Master Artist*, edited by Ernest N. Emenyonu, Trenton, NJ: Africa World Press, Inc., 2004, pp. 49–63. Copyright © 2004 Ernest N. Emenyonu. All rights reserved. Reproduced by permission.

mention only these few. The Umuofia community of *Things Fall Apart* being a close-knit one, each man is known along with his foibles, weaknesses and strengths, all of these attributes and qualities force the kind of personality and/or power he can muster at any gathering. When he speaks, such a man by his gestures, stance, posture and gaze is forced to live up to community expectations without appearing strange or incoherent to himself or his community. . . .

Four selected dialogues involving some of the more notable characters in the novel would help us understand better the dynamics of power in the community of Umuofia.

Unoka Uses a Proverb to Gain Power

Background information on Unoka as a youth and an old man reveals that, in contrast to his son, Okonkwo, even as a youth, Unoka was "lazy and imprudent and was quite incapable of thinking about tomorrow". He spent the meager money he had drinking palm-wine and making merry. He was, therefore, a debtor who was despised by his community. His demeanor reflects his good-for-nothing life, for he wore a "haggard and mournful look," except when he was playing his flute. He was thus a "failure" as a grown-up. He was "poor and his wife and children had barely enough to eat." He was a "loafer" and a "coward".

The encounter between wily Unoka and dignified Okoye, who "had a large barn full of yams and had three wives" and was about to take the "idemili title," the third highest title in the land, sways the reader inadvertently to Okoye's side. Human beings are such that with conditioning they imbibe the values of the community and culture they live in. A well-entrenched and established citizen is certainly more beneficial to a community than a loafer and a drunkard. However, by the end of their encounter, Unoka had succeeded in turning the table against Okoye, making him out as silly and ineffective at best, at worst a Shylock, the proverbial oppressor, who has come to demand his "pound of flesh:"

> As soon as Unoka understood what his friend was driving at, he burst out laughing. He laughed loud and long and his voice rang out clear as the ogene, and tears stood in his eyes. His visitor was amazed, and sat speechless. At the end, Unoka was able to give an answer between fresh outbursts of mirth.

> "Look at that wall," he said. . . . "Look at those lines of chalk". . . . Unoka had a sense of the dramatic and so he allowed a pause, in which he took a pinch of snuff and sneezed noisily, and then he continued: "Each group there represents a debt to someone, and each stroke is one hundred cowries [shells used for money]. You see, I owe that man a thousand cowries, but he has not come to wake me up in the morning for it. I shall pay you, but not today. Our elders say that the sun will shine on those who stand before it shines on those who kneel under them. I shall pay my big debts first." And he took another pinch of snuff, as if that was paying the big debts first. Okoye rolled his goatskin and departed.

Unoka outwitted Okoye by exercising physical ability, power through the length and timbre of his outbursts of laughter, the ring of his voice, his dramatic presentation of the case and above all the clinching of the whole episode with a very apt proverb. It is important to recall that among the Igbo, proverbs are "the palm-oil with which words are eaten".

Colonizers Use Language to Defeat Igbo Men

Compared to his predecessor, Mr. Brown, the new white, British administrator, Mr. Smith, is not liked, because he treats Africans and their gods with contempt. Some overzealous converts to the new Christian religion unmask the *egwugwu* in protest against African religion. When the group of six men destroy the new Christian church building in retaliation, they are invited into the presence of the District Commissioner, ostensibly for dialogue. But, the cunning administrator tactically "disarms" the community leaders before they have a chance to unsheathe their machetes, that is assuming they are even in the disposition to wage a battle against the administrator. Here is the process of his display of power. First of all, the Commissioner gets the group of six men to trust him and so put down their guard by coming in alone and sitting down. Secondly, he invites their spokesperson to tell him the group's version of what had happened between the villagers and the agents of the British colonial administration. As Ogbuefi Ekuweme, the leader of the group, rises to his feet to give his deposition, the Commissioner interrupts him, thus stressing that he, the Commissioner, is the power broker. He gives power of speech and takes it back at will. It turns out he wants to bring in his men at that point, again ostensibly to be privy to the dialogue, so that there would be no further mistakes. How would the group of six men have known that his real intention was to have them bound up and that he had no need to hear their side of the case? All becomes clear to them when they are surrounded and hand-cuffed. To hand-cuff a man is to impose one's ultimate physical power on his person. He loses all ability to use his limbs. Even running any great distance in hand-cuffs is a near impossibility. Then the administrator moves methodically to the next stage. Having emasculated the men, he is no longer pleading, or feigning to plead. He is again the agent of the Queen of England whose Britannica rules the waves:

> We shall not do you any harm . . . , if only you agree to co-operate with us. We have brought a peaceful administration to you and your people so that you may be happy. If any man ill-treats you we shall come to your rescue. But we will not allow you to ill-treat others. We have a court of law where we judge cases and administer justice just as it is done in our own country under a great queen. I have

> brought you here because you joined together to molest others, to burn people's houses and their place of worship. That must not happen in the dominion of the queen, the most powerful ruler in the world. I have decided that you will pay a fine of two hundred bags of cowries. You will be released as soon as you agree to this and undertake to collect that fine from your people. What do you say to that?

> The six men remained sullen and silent and the Commissioner left them for a while.

The District Commissioner finishes his address by imposing a fine on the six men, which he expects them to collect from their people by themselves or face worse treatments. The six are undoubtedly dumb-founded at the realization, in the end, of how a single man has been able to overpower a group. His African agents, the court messengers, follow-up on their master's footsteps, confirming [Marxist philosophers Antonio] Gramsci and [Louis] Althusser's ideologies on how members of a group embrace the tactics of the oppressor and inadvertently foster his aggression even against themselves as a distinct group. They shaved the men's hair, beat them and taunted them: "Who is the chief among you? . . . We see that every pauper wears the anklet of title in Umuofia. Does it cost as much as ten cowries?". The group's only recourse was silence and hunger strike. Even when they are left alone by the Commissioner's men "they found no words to speak to one another", until they were tired and had to give in to save themselves further torture. When the ordeal of the six finally filtered down to their subjects, "Umuofia was like a startled animal with ears erect, sniffing the silent, ominous air and not knowing which way to run". It is significant that even the community's reaction was only defensive, not aggressive. They were minded only to see "which way to run." By subduing the leaders of the group, the Commissioner has subdued the entire community of Umuofia. . . .

Using Speech to Convey Knowledge

Following the detention of the group of six, Okika, one of them, seethes with anger. This opportunistic emotion transforms his words into a veritable fire of words, as he breathes fire and promises death to the perpetrators of the heinous misdeed. Okika, unlike Egonwanne, the oldest man of the village who would have toed the path of compromise, wanted to match power with power, might with might. Onyeka, who had a "booming voice" was asked to clear the stage for him, for even though he was a great orator, he was not blessed with a booming voice. Okika's speech is a veritable classic of rhetoric, and we see the need to cite it in its entirety, so that the stages of his power of language on the people may become clear:

> You all know why we are here, when we ought to be building our barns or mending our huts, when we should be putting our compounds in order. My father used to say to me: "Whenever you see a toad jumping in broad daylight, then know that something is after its life." When I saw you all pouring into this meeting from all the quarters of our clan so early in the morning, I knew that something was after our life." He paused for a brief moment and then began again:
>
> All our gods are weeping. Idemili is weeping, Ogwugwu is weeping, Agbala is weeping, and all the others. Our dead fathers are weeping because of the shameful sacrilege they are suffering and the abomination we have all seen with our eyes." He stopped again to steady his trembling voice.
>
> This is a great gathering. No clan can boast of greater numbers or greater valor. But are we all here? I ask you: Are all the sons of Umuofia with us here?" A deep murmur swept through the crowd. They are not. . . . They have broken the clan and gone their several ways. We who are here this morning have remained true to our fathers, but our brothers have deserted us and joined a stranger to soil their fatherland. If we fight the stranger we shall hit our brothers and perhaps

shed the blood of a clansman. But we must do it. Our fathers never dreamed of such a thing, they never killed their brothers. But a white man never came to them. So we must do what our fathers would have done. Eneke the bird was asked why he was always on the wing and he replied: "Men have learned to shoot without missing their mark and I have learned to fly without perching on a twig." We must root out this evil. And if our brothers take the side of evil we must root them out too. And we must do it now. We must bail this water now that it is only ankle-deep . . ."

Having sensitized the gathering to the emergent nature of the situation, Okika does not waste time but goes on, employing run-on phrases. Then the first pause. He allows the people to internalize what he just told them. When he begins to speak again, he bemoans the sacrilegious nature of the offense, adding that in the face of adversity, the community has not seen it fit to stand together. The inference is that a house divided unto itself cannot stand. He intones that the forefathers whose presence is eternally with the living would not have condoned such an act. As worthy descendants of the ancestors, they should do what their forebears would have done. It is significant that most Igbo proverbs begin with "As our fathers say." At this stage, Okika begins to lay the ground rules for action. It is almost as if he was saying, "But we must do it," "So we must do what our fathers would have done," "We must root them out too."

Okika has a lot of ability power, power of demeanor and knowledge. He knows how to pick the right words and work effectively on the psychology of his audience. When five court messengers of the British administration showed up to interrupt the gathering, charging that, "The white man whose power you know too well has ordered this meeting to stop," Okonkwo was ready for action, to counter indirect coercive power with direct coercive power:

In a flash Okonkwo drew his machete. The messenger crouched to avoid the blow. It was useless, Okonkwo's machete descended twice and the man's head lay beside his uniformed body.

Obierika Uses Language to Reverse Roles

The four escaping agents of the British Commissioner report to their master the murder of one of them by Okonkwo. Enraged, the Commissioner comes down from Government Hill to seek redress:

> 'Which among you is called Okonkwo?' he asked through his interpreter.
>
> 'He is not here,' replied Obierika.
>
> 'Where is he?'
>
> 'He is not here!'

The Commissioner becomes visibly angry. In spite of the apparent dichotomy in the degree of social power, in the end, we can say that it is a perfect power match. First of all, Obierika refuses, right from the start, to volunteer more information than is necessary to respond to the Commissioner's question without appearing to be disrespectful. This tactic is not lost on the Commissioner who begins to be irritated: "Where is he?" he asks in reply to Obierika's non-committal first response: "He is not here." Following the repeat of this same statement, the Commissioner loses total control of his temper. He warns that there will be adverse consequences to disobedience of his orders. At that point, Obierika recognizes the danger in prolonging his register. He thus changes his strategy, although still determined to match power with power. "We can take you where he is, and perhaps your men will help us." The British commissioner finds Obierika's circumlocution very annoying. Beaten in his own game, he leads a band of men into the bush where he finds Okonkwo hanging on his suicide rope. It is a total defeat for the Commissioner who would never get to arrest his victim and punish him at will. Obierika feels triumphant for he recognizes that Okonkwo, his friend, has escaped the commissioner's wrath through suicide. He rubs salt into injury when he asks the commissioner and his men, lumping them together as strangers to the land and instruments of the oppression of the people, to help them take down the dead body:

> Perhaps your men can help us bring him down and bury him. We have sent for strangers from another village to do it for us, but they may be a long time coming.

By casting the commissioner and his men as the Other, Obierika has de-centered power, moving it to the margin. He has successfully negotiated ideological power, turning it on its head. With great ability, knowledge and demeanor, Obierika has reversed the roles of the master and the subaltern [subordinate], putting the subaltern, albeit temporarily, over the master.

Women Play a Key Role in the Community Depicted in *Things Fall Apart*

Linda Strong-Leek

Linda Strong-Leek holds a PhD from Michigan State University and is associate professor of Women's Studies and General Studies at Berea College in Kentucky. In 2009, she published Excising the Spirit: A Literary Analysis of Female Circumcision.

Strong-Leek asserts in this selection that a reading of Things Fall Apart *from a woman's perspective provides insight into the pivotal role women play in the Igbo community. She states that male critics identify strongly with Okonkwo, thus overlooking important women such as Ekwefi, Ezinma, and Ojuigo. Women, too, must change their biases by acknowledging their indoctrination to the patriarchal world view. As childbearers, Strong-Leek points out, women are important to the survival of the community. Even Okonkwo acknowledges the importance of his beloved child, Ezinma, by following her into the forest.*

Before beginning this feminist analysis, we must review the historical and cultural context in which *Things Fall Apart* was written. *Things Fall Apart*, first published in 1958, was initially written as a response to colonialist representations of Africa and Africans in literature, specifically Joyce Cary's *Mister Johnson* (1939). Cary's work positions Africans in the typical colonialist frame: as individuals without motives, forethought, or knowledge other than base responses to their environs. As [literary critic Abdul] Jan Mohammed states, "colonial literature is an exploration of a world at the boundaries of civiliza-

Linda Strong-Leek, "Reading as a Woman: Chinua Achebe's *Things Fall Apart* and Feminist Criticism," *African Studies Quarterly*, vol. 5, no. 2, 2001. Reproduced by permission. http://web.africa.ufl.edu/asq/v5/v5i2a2.htm.

tion; a world that has not (yet) been domesticated by European signification." It is a world perceived as "uncontrollable, chaotic, unattainable, and ultimately evil." Against this context, Achebe's novel allowed European readers to perceive Africans through an alternate lens. The Igbo society described by Achebe has definitive and complex social systems, values and traditions. Achebe presents customs such as the abandonment of multiple birth babies and the sacrifice of human beings as conventions and not barbaric, inhumane rituals. He brilliantly places his characters within an ancient civilization with a labyrinthine system of governance and laws.

Cultural Norms of African Life

Consequently, Achebe's main character, Okonkwo, emerges early in the text as a traditional hero, who has within himself the ability to languish or attain his goals. Achebe's readers understand that European colonialists do not precipitate Okonkwo's ultimate downfall. Instead, it is Okonkwo's seeds of self-destruction, which are deeply concealed in his desire to be the antithesis of his "feminine" father.

Moreover, though Achebe's text is written in English, the language of the colonizer, it remains authentically African. . . . The actions, ethos, and characterizations in the text depict a culture in transition, with indigenous practices which may be perceived as untenable to foreigners, but which are [ordinarily] accepted within. Even when certain members of the community seek refuge in the Christian church, it is most often because they find themselves casualties of specific cultural norms: women who have multiple births, albinos, etc. . . . rather than those who are secure in the traditional world.

Depth of Major Female Characters

In addition, as [literary critic Solomon] Iyasere states, reading Achebe's conventional world as a woman, one cannot merely ascribe to the view that "one of Achebe's great achievements is his ability to keep alive our sympathy for Okonkwo despite the moral revulsion from some of his violent, inhuman acts." Instead, query whether this sympathy may remain intact for those reading through a feminist lens. Although many critics explicate upon the horrors and injustices Okonkwo inflicts upon the men in his life (mainly his son Nwoye, his other "son" Ikemefuna), most omit any discussion of the abuse suffered by Okonkwo's wives. However, this critique reevaluates the significance of not only the pain of these women, but also their importance as individuals within their community. Therefore, [in the words of critic Jonathan Culler] "by providing a different point of departure (this feminist reading) brings into focus the identification of male critics with one character and permits the analysis of male misreadings." Hence, this work challenges these misreadings and positions the female characters at the center of the text. Instead of focusing on Okonkwo, as most critics have, this reading is focused on two major female characters, Ekwefi and Ezinma, and one minor figure, Ojiugo. They are mentioned only briefly, if at all, by other critics of the text, and when referred to, are examined only in relation to Okonkwo's actions or motivations. Reading this text as a woman, this author analyzes these characters according to their self-perceptions, as well as societal awareness of them as women, wives, mothers and daughters. Exploring the relationships between these women reveals not only alliances between mothers and their offspring, but also alliances between comrades in arms.

The characterization of Ekwefi, Okonkwo's second wife, almost seems insignificant to one reading from a patriarchal standpoint, but when reevaluated, one will find that she is a well of knowledge, love, and fierce independence. Ekwefi has endured much heartache and stigmatism. In *Things Fall Apart* women are viewed mainly as child bearers and help mates for their husbands. Due to the phallocentric [penis-centered] notion that women must produce many hardy, male progenies to be valued within their cultural milieu, Ekwefi is considered a cursed woman because after ten live births, only one child—a daughter—survives. Thus, "By the time Onwumbiko was born, Ekwefi was a very bitter woman." Accordingly, she resents the good fortune of the first wife: her ability to produce healthy, strong male children. . . . The conventional perspective of most readings of this text is that Ekwefi has been debilitated by life's harsh circumstances. However, instead of continuing to lament her adversity, Ekwefi devotes her time and energy to the one child who does live, and finds solace in her relationship with her daughter.

Pivotal Role as Child Bearers

While male readings indicate that "the man is the point of reference in this society" [literary critic Eustace] Palmer stresses that as child bearers, women are pivotal to the literal survival of community and societal norms. After the death of her second child, it is Okonkwo, not Ekwefi, who consults the dibia to locate the source of her difficulty. It is also Okonkwo who confers with yet another dibia after the death of Ekwefi's third child, highlighting Palmer's contention that Ekwefi has failed not because she cannot have a viable child, but because she cannot provide her husband with male progeny who would, then, carry on in his father's name. Okonkwo is concerned about the deaths of the children, but impervious to Ekwefi's privation. No one comforts Ekwefi as she is forced to watch the dibia mutilate her child, drag him through the streets by his ankles, and finally lay him to rest in the Evil Forest with other obanje children [children believed to be evil spirits] and outcasts. It is significant, though, that Okonkwo does demonstrate concern for the female child, Ezinma, as he follows her into the forest after she is taken by the Priestess, Chielo.

No Compassion for Brutality to Women

Moreover, most readings of the novel do not address the brutal beating Ekwefi receives at the hands of Okonkwo: "Who killed this banana tree?" He asked. A hush fell over the compound immediately . . . Without further argument Okonkwo gave her a sound beating and left her and her only daughter weeping. The novel continues with a brief discussion of this continued abuse later when Okonkwo threatens Ekwefi with a gun after hearing her murmur under her breath. Yet, the next day, the New Yam Festival continues without a public outcry for this battered woman. Reading as a woman, one may understand Ekwefi's resignation, as she recalls how she came to be Okonkwo's second wife:

> Many years ago when she was the village beauty Okonkwo had won her heart by throwing the Cat in the greatest contest within living memory. She did not marry him then because he was too poor to pay her bride-price. But a few years later she ran away from her husband and came to live with Okonkwo.

Culler writes that "women's experience, many feminist critics claim, will lead them to value works differently from their male counterparts, who may regard the problems women characteristically encounter as of limited interest." Therefore, although a male critic may deem these events as minor instances, the feminist reader must note that there is, in these passages, a great sense of irony and regret. Preparing to attend her favorite pastime, the annual wrestling event, Ekwefi recollects her great love for the then impoverished Okonkwo. Although she was married to another man, Ekwefi's desire for Okonkwo is so great that at the first opportunity she abandons her husband to be with him, yet a sound beating is the compensation she receives for her love and devotion. Although this brutality does not warrant any attention from the elders, Okonkwo's flogging of his youngest wife, Ojiugo, does. There is a public outcry, not because of the physical battering, but, rather the timing of the occurrence—The Week of Peace: "'You have committed a great evil' . . . It was the first time for many years that a man had broken the sacred peace. Even the oldest men could only remember one or two other occasions somewhere in the dim past." Iyasere notes "the peace of the tribe as a whole takes precedence over personal considerations." He could have continued, elaborating that particularly in reference to women, the unanimity of the patriarchy is the main priority of the community, rather than the physical safety of its women.

Furthermore, there is no regard from the elders about Ojiugo's condition; to the contrary, one elder boldly asserts that she is at fault, and thus, the beating itself is not the point of contention. Moreover, because Ekwefi is beaten after this week, there is no outrage beyond the intercession of the other two wives who dare say in support of their wounded sister, "It is enough." Communal events merely continue as normal. The great fight is fought, and new wrestling heroes are born. One may also wonder if while reflecting upon her life, Ekwefi is pondering the life of another young woman who has just decided that the new wrestling hero will become her husband, and the possible ramifications of such a decision. However, since Ojiugo is battered during the sacred week, Okonkwo must make a sacrifice to the earth goddess to recompense for himself and the community, which may be punished because of his dishonorable deed.

Culler notes that one strategy in the attempt to read as a woman is to "take an author's ideas seriously when . . . they wish to be taken seriously." If one is to take *Things Fall Apart* seriously, one must question a society that has no compassion for the brutality that is omnipresent in the lives of Okonkwo's wives. The reader must also question the patriarchal notion that devalues women so much that their feelings are not significant. There is, moreover, no week or even day of peace for the women of Umuofia. They cannot find sanctuary within the confines of their own homes, or in the arms of their own husbands.

Three Igbo women dressed in traditional clothes for a special occasion. © David Simpson/
Eye Ubiquitous/Alamy.

Ezinma Treated Differently

There is one woman, or young girl, who elicits pure love from
all the lives she touches, even her father, Okonkwo. However,
he cannot fully appreciate Ezinma as a person. Instead of ad-
miring her for her strength and disposition as a burgeoning
woman, Okonkwo is saddened by the fact that she is not
male.

Ezinma is Ekwefi's only living child, and it is demonstrated that her father does in fact respect her character. When
Okonkwo acknowledges these affections, a male reading may
solicit a sense of alliance with him and wish, for his sake, that
Ezinma were male: "She should have been a boy, he thought
as he looked at his ten-year-old daughter . . . If Ezinma had
been a boy I would have been happier. She has the right spirit."
Reading the text from the male purview, one may empathize
with Okonkwo who, because of the fates, has no child, except
a daughter, worthy of conveying familial legacies. But because
Ezinma is female, she cannot function in this capacity. More-

over, even a woman, in a traditional reading of the text would support this notion. Culler articulates that "what feminists ignore or deny at their peril . . . is that women share men's anti-female feelings—usually in a mitigated form, but deeply nevertheless." According to Culler this stems partly from the fact that women "have been steeped in self-derogatory societal stereotypes," while being constantly "pitted against each other for the favors of the reigning sex. . . ." While reading as a woman, one must acknowledge that women are also indoctrinated to envision the world from a patriarchal perspective, and that, in Ezinma's case, one must revise these biases to appreciate her strength, singularity and vivacity.

Initially believed to be an obanje child who had only come to stay for a short period, after Ezinma thrives, she is pampered by her mother, and as the child who would be king if she were male. Ezinma is the embodiment of all the women in this novel represent: intelligence, vitality, and fortitude. Even in her relationship with her mother, Ezinma exhibits what Okonkwo, through his phallocentric lens, perceives as masculine tendencies:

> Ezinma did not call her mother Nne like all children. She called her by her name, Ekwefi, as her father and other grown-up people did. The relationship between them was not only that of mother and child. There was something in it like the companionship of equals, which was strengthened by such little conspiracies as eating eggs in the bedroom.

A Special Bond

Ezinma calls her mother by her name, signifying the development of an autonomous, effectual being. Ezinma and Ekwefi share a bond that is unlike most other parental ties in the novel: they are virtually equals. Their affiliation is based on mutual love, respect, and understanding. They share secret moments, such as eating eggs in the confines of her bedroom (eggs are considered a delicacy), solidifying their esprit de corps, even after Okonkwo threatens them both. Culler notes that when analyzing one's position as a female reader, "Critics identify (the) fear that female solidarity threatens male dominance and the male character." Thus, this maternal connection becomes a caveat for Okonkwo and traditional society because he cannot control the depths of love and the shared enthusiasm between mother and daughter. This is most evident when, for example, Okonkwo forbids Ekwefi to leave her hut after Ezinma is carried off by the chief priestess. Ekwefi ignores her husband and risks a flogging to follow Chielo and her daughter throughout the night, until she is certain that her daughter will return home safely. When Okonkwo asks, "Where are you going?" Ekwefi boldly asserts that she is following Chielo. But instead of attempting to detain her, Okonkwo joins the journey, following from a safe distance, also to ensure the safety of his beloved child. This mother/daughter alliance is explicated throughout the text, though there is little discussion of it in most analyses of the novel.

One must acknowledge as well that male and female roles are societal constructs, and thus, the entire female identity is based more upon societal constraints rather than physiological realities. Women are taught to mother, while men are conditioned to dominate and control. Hence, we know that men may also read as women, if they are willing to rethink their positions, as well as women's positions within patriarchal constructs. . . .

As this constructed woman reader analyzes the characters of Ekwefi, Ojiugo, and Ezinma as major figures whose lives are not just affected by the whims of their father/husband, but also as women who affect their husband/father and each other, I believe that only when one consciously attempts to read as a woman, these formerly peripheral characters may be afforded proper critical attention by male/female readers of this great African novel.

Achebe Does Not Idealize Precolonial and Postcolonial Igbo Society

G.D. Killam

G.D. Killam has written extensively on African literature, with special emphasis on the works of Chinua Achebe. He is University Professor Emeritus in the School of English and Theatre Studies at the University of Guelph, Canada, where he formerly was professor of Commonwealth and African Literature. He has also taught in several African nations.

In the following selection, Killam states that Achebe is able to view the Igbo (also spelled Ibo) society objectively, and does not idealize the forces that led to destruction of their way of life. The past is not presented as eternally benign, and the colonizing era is not all negative. Using simple and almost casual prose, Achebe manages to portray the intensity of Igbo life and the changes the community endures. Killam believes the story of the white man's coming and its effect on the Igbo is told without sentimentality.

*T*hings Fall Apart is a vision of what life was like in Iboland between 1850 and 1900. Achebe makes a serious attempt to capture realistically the strains and tensions of the experiences of Ibo people under the impact of colonialism. What ultimately gives this novel its strength is Achebe's feelings for the plight and problems of these peoples. It is not wholly true, however, to say that the novel is written consistently from their point of view. Achebe is a twentieth-century Ibo man, a de-colonized writer, and recognizes the wide gulf which exists between his present-day society and that of Ibo villagers sixty years ago, sixty years which have seen remarkable changes in the texture and structure of Ibo society.

Achebe Is an Objective Writer

Achebe is able to view objectively the forces which irresistibly and inevitably destroyed traditional Ibo social ties and with them the quality of Ibo life. In showing Ibo society before and after the coming of the white man he avoids the temptation to present the past as idealized and the present as ugly and unsatisfactory. The atmosphere of the novel is realistic and not romantic, although there are romantic elements in it. Put another way, Achebe manages to express a romantic vision of Ibo life in realistic form, to encompass aspects of that life which evoke it in all its complexity and convincingness. Achebe's success proceeds not from his interest in the history of his people and their folklore and legend in an academic sense, even though he puts these to good use in the novel, nor from the fact that he tells a compelling story, although this is true. His success proceeds from his ability to create a sense of real life and real issues in the book and to see his subject from a point of view which is neither idealistic nor dishonest. Of the temptation to present the past in an idealized form, especially to the African writer, Achebe has written:

> ... the past needs to be recreated not only for the enlightenment of our detractors but even more for our own education. Because ... the past with all its imperfections, never lacked dignity. ... This is where the writer's integrity comes in. Will he be strong enough to overcome the temptation to select only those facts which flatter him? If he succumbs he will have branded himself as an untrustworthy witness. But it is not only his personal integrity as an artist which is involved. The credibility of the world he is attempting to recreate will be called to question and he will defeat his own purpose if he is suspected of glossing over inconvenient facts.

Things Fall Apart is a small book which for all its apparent casualness and sobriety of style and the complexity of the human relationships it presents, is a very well-constructed book, in which technical problems of presentation have been most carefully worked out. Further, Achebe's method of working affects complete verisimilitude in its presentation: he never imposes himself between us and the scene he presents. Achebe is the most objective of writers in this sense.

Casual Style Contrasts with Intensity of Events

Things Fall Apart has three sections or parts to it: the first and most important is set in Umuofia before the coming of the white man—before his existence is even known. The second part dramatizes Okonkwo's banishment to Mbanta, the village of his mother's people, for sins committed against the Earth Goddess, and describes, mostly through reports, the coming of the white man to the nine villages and the establishment of an alien church, government and trading system and the gradual encroachment of these on the traditional patterns of tribal life. The third section and the shortest brings the novel swiftly to a close, dramatizing the death of the old ways and the death of Okonkwo.

Achebe's prose has been described as 'leisurely' and 'stately' and a casual reading of the book, especially the first part, supports such judgement. Because Achebe refuses to take sides in the issues he describes and dramatizes, his presentation is disinterested and this quality is reflected in the writing. Yet, restrained as the pace may be, it moves the story forward with a sense of inevitability, the momentum gradually increasing until the first climax is reached: Okonkwo's third sin against the Earth Goddess and his subsequent banishment. The casual approach and style quite belie the intensity of the life the novel evokes and from the outset Achebe's absolute certainty of approach is established. Umuofia is an organic unity. It is a place where people live, a community, a centre of co-operating and conflicting men and women, which achieves an identity of its own. Moreover, it is unified by an Ibo consciousness and achieves a rich ambiguity which refers ultimately not only to Umuofia and the nine villages but to all of Iboland at this particular point in time.

Okonkwo Embodies Ibo Values

At the centre of the community is Okonkwo, a character of intense individuality, yet one in whom the values most admired by Ibo people are consolidated. He is both an individual and a type. . . .

Okonkwo was 'one of the greatest men of his time', the embodiment of Ibo values, the man who better than most symbolized his race. His stature is presented as heroic. His story, as was mentioned above, is presented in terms which resemble those of Aristotelian tragedy—the working out in the life of a hero of industry, courage and eminence, of an insistent fatality (in this book symbolized by the *chi*, or personal god) which transcends his ability to fully understand or resist a fore-ordained sequence of events. Achebe suggests as well the flaw, or flaws in his nature—his inordinate ambition and his refusal to tolerate anything less than excellence, taken in conjunction with an impulsive rage to which he easily gives way and which produces irrational responses to situations. In this connection the comment that Okonkwo had 'no patience with his father' is important, for Unoka, the father, represents everything which Okonkwo personally despises and his life embodies the antithesis of those values most cherished by the Ibo people. We are told that Unoka was 'poor and his wife and children had barely enough to eat', that he was 'lazy and improvident', a 'debtor' and a 'coward who could not stand the sight of blood'. Achebe characterizes him deftly in this passage:

[Unoka] would remember his own childhood, how he had often wandered around looking for a kite sailing leisurely against the blue sky. As soon as he found one he would sing with his whole being, welcoming it back from its long, long journey, and asking it if it had brought home any lengths of cloth.

His capacity to day-dream, his laziness and improvidence—his childish hope that the kite would bring back cloth and thus absolve him from the necessity of providing for himself—are summed up in this anecdote, which is not without charm, and his character is made to stand in direct contrast to Okonkwo's and to enhance his central position in the book. This is made explicit in the second chapter of the book:

> [Okonkwo's] whole life was dominated by fear, the fear of failure and weakness. It was deeper and more intimate than the fear of evil and capricious gods and of magic, the fear of the forest and of the forces of nature, malevolent, red in tooth and claw. Okonkwo's fear was greater than these. It was not external but lay deep within himself. It was the fear of himself, lest he should be found to resemble his father. Even as a little boy he had resented his father's failure and weakness, and even now he still remembered how he had suffered when a playmate told him that his father was *agbala*. That was how Okonkwo first came to know that a *agbala* was not only another name for a woman, it could also mean a man who had taken no title. And so Okonkwo was ruled by one passion—to hate everything that his father Unoka had loved. One of those things was gentleness and another was idleness.

The passages cited above suggest Achebe's sensitive yet unobtrusive use of English to reflect the African environment and to integrate character and incident through the use of imagery drawn from traditional sources, a technique so consistent in its application that it can be demonstrated in passages taken from any part of the novel. . . .

Violent Customs Portrayed Without Judgment

Okonkwo's downfall and eventual banishment from the tribe at the end of the first part of the novel proceeds from offences committed 'against the earth'. The first occurs during a week of peace when he beats his wife for her fecklessness. Characteristically impulsive, Okonkwo was not one to let fear of a goddess stand in his way. For this offence Ani demands retribution in the form of money which Okonkwo pays. The second offence relates to the killing of Ikemefuna, a boy-hostage taken from a neighbouring clan and placed in Okonkwo's household. Ikemefuna becomes as a son to Okonkwo. Nwoye, Okonkwo's eldest son and a source of grave concern to Okonkwo because he shows all the signs of possessing the 'female' disposition of his grandfather, thrives under the influence of Ikemefuna—Nwoye, we are told, 'grows like a yam tendril in the rainy season'. The deity eventually decrees that Ikemefuna must be killed. Okonkwo is warned that he must take no hand in the killing. Yet for fear of appearing weak and cowardly Okonkwo cuts down Ikemefuna with his machete. . . .

The scene is rendered by Achebe with a terseness which makes the horror of it all the more compelling. Yet the special horror is, not that Okonkwo has killed this boy whom he has grown to love—the authority and decision of the Oracle are not questioned—but, as Okonkwo's friend Obierika says with a voice prophetic of the doom which will overtake Okonkwo, his is the 'kind of action for which the goddess wipes out whole families'. . . .

Arrival of Colonizers Told with Restraint

Achebe tells the story of the coming of the white men—at first the missionaries and then, close behind, the civil administrators, soldiers and traders—with characteristic economy and restraint which belie the complexity of the issues involved, a complexity which is directly reflected in the structure of the novel. Obierika makes two visits to Okonkwo during the latter's exile. During the first visit he reveals, almost casually, that Abame, one of the villages in the union of the nine villages, 'is no more'. Recording the tale of refugees who had come to Umuofia from Abame Obierika says:

'During the last planting season a white man had appeared in their clan.'

'An albino,' suggested Okonkwo.

'He was not an albino. He was quite different.' He sipped his wine. 'And he was riding an iron horse. The first people who saw him ran away, but he stood beckoning to them. In the end the fearless ones went near and even touched him. The elders consulted their Oracle and it told them that the strange man would break their clan and spread destruction among them.' Obierika again drank a little of his wine. 'And so they killed the white man and tied his iron horse to their sacred tree because it looked as if it would run away to call the man's friends. I forgot to tell you another thing which the Oracle said. It said that other white men were on their way. They were locusts, it said, and that first man was their harbinger sent to explore the terrain. . . . Anyway . . . they killed him and tied up his iron horse. . . .

Here again the consistency of Achebe's approach to his art is revealed. The image of the 'iron horse' (a bicycle) is central for through its use Achebe is able to suggest the differences in ideas and understanding which existed between the two systems by presenting them in the idiom of the Ibo people. In this way he is able to prepare the way for showing the lack of understanding which will characterize his elaboration of the wider ideological beliefs between the two systems. . . .

Traditional Balance Upset

It is not the alien religion [of the white man] which accounts for the destruction of the old ways and causes them to fall apart. Rather it is a combination of factors, one of which is the new religion, the other of which is trade. The new faith possesses an appeal sufficiently strong to challenge and undermine the old religion. At the same time, through the incentives of the new value placed on palm-oil and palm kernels, the acquisitive nature of the society gains precedence. The traditional balance is upset. The male principle of acquisitiveness for the first time gains precedence over the female which heretofore provided the ethical and moral basis of conduct and acted as a restraint on the male principle. . . .

Things Fall Apart is the expression in terms of imaginative art of the tensions, stresses and conflicts, presented in personal, social and spiritual terms, of late nineteenth-century Ibo society. The men and women in the novel are real, they live in the world and seek to control their destinies, sometimes successfully, sometimes painfully and with difficulty and error. The inevitable processes of history are suggested by the struggle made concrete in the novel and conceived and presented in actual and particular terms, without idealism and without sentimentality.

Igbo and European Cultures Clash

Willene P. Taylor

Willene P. Taylor is professor of English in the Center for African and African-American Studies at Southern University at New Orleans. She has written literary criticism for numerous academic journals.

Taylor states in the following selection that the Igbo (spelled here Ibo) must search for values in a world that is constantly changing. The entire clan is threatened by a force—the colonizers—that seeks to impose values that are alien to the Igbo way of life. Okonkwo is the individual personification of this conflict. The white missionaries work to disarm the Igbo with a soft approach to subverting their culture. The district commissioner, Taylor notes, displays a much less subtle attitude that betrays his ethnocentrism and his insensitivity toward the Igbo way of life.

One of the main themes in Chinua Achebe's novel, *Things Fall Apart*, is the search for values in a world that is constantly beset by change. Having taken his title from William Butler Yeats' poem, "The Second Coming," Achebe, like Yeats, presents in vivid terms his interpretation of the cyclical view of history. . . . The first of Achebe's cycles, Ibo tribal life before the coming of the British to Nigeria near the end of the nineteenth century, makes way for the beginning of twentieth century Europeanization of Africa with all its implied consequences for still another era—the future of post-colonial Africa.

Willene P. Taylor, "The Search for Values Theme in Chinua Achebe's Novel *Things Fall Apart*: A Crisis of the Soul," in *Understanding "Things Fall Apart": Selected Essays and Criticism*, edited by Solomon O. Iyasere, Albany, NY: The Whitson Publishing Company, 1998, pp. 27–39. Copyright © 1998 Solomon O. Iyasere. Reproduced by permission of the author.

In using Yeats' European material to draw a contrast between the various periods of Ibo history, Achebe is able to accomplish two things. First of all, through manipulating the Yeatsian theme about the changes inevitable in human history, the novelist succeeds in showing that the sense of historical decay, continuity, and rebirth is not only characteristic of the European tradition but also of the African tradition. Second, by exploiting this European literature and historiography, ironically Achebe is able to reverse the white man's narrow definition of culture and history.

A Clan Threatened by Alien Values

On one level of *Things Fall Apart*, the novelist depicts the plight of the protagonist Okonkwo, the character most opposed to change, in trying to hold on to the traditional values of his society amidst the imposition of a powerful, alien force that seeks to undermine these values and practices. On still another level, and perhaps more importantly, the novelist depicts the predicament of the entire clan in preserving these values when they become threatened by another and more puissant [powerful] way of life. . . .

Achebe grew up at a time when Africans were beginning to oppose European rule through political action and were also beginning to question with increasing vigor and clarity the cultural assumptions used to justify that rule. Hence, the novelist began to question and to object to the demeaning portrait of the African depicted in the novels of [Joseph] Conrad and [Joyce] Cary. . . .

A View of Ibo Life

Section one of the novel is highly anthropological but sets the stage for the conflict in values in the last half of the work. As [literary critic] Charles Larson has suggested, this tension is introduced early in the novel "because the old African way of life typified by Okonkwo, is unable to adapt to the new, to the

West." . . . The narrative is weighted down with ethnological material, which makes the reading plod along rather wearily, unlike the latter section of the novel which moves rather swiftly to a climax. This weightiness of the narrative in the first part of the work is due not so much to Achebe's lack of narrative skill, but to his successful attempt to carry out his initial purpose; that is, to show that the traditional life and value system of this rather rigorously ordered and secure African society will fall apart when it becomes exposed to western influences, represented by Christianity and the British colonial rule. Also, the lack of a readily apparent plot in Part I allows Achebe to give a detailed catalogue of Ibo values and customs and relate them not only to Okonkwo, the main character, but also simultaneously to members of Okonkwo's Umuofian clan.

Okonkwo Overcompensates

When the novel begins, the reader is immediately told of the values revered and respected by the Ibo people. For example, "Age was respected among his people," the narrator states, "but achievement was revered." It is just this emphasis on achievement that leads Okonkwo, the protagonist of the book, to become obsessed with the weakness in his father Unoka—an obsession so strong that it becomes the ruling force of his entire being. . . .

Okonkwo becomes so obsessed with his father's weakness and with demonstrating his own perceived superior masculinity that, indeed, the reader is not surprised when this masculinity later turns out to take the forms of child-abuse and wife-beating, the latter having happened during the Week of Peace. And although beating one's wife during the Week of Peace can bring destruction to this intradependent and tightly knit clan, it makes little difference to Okonkwo, who is excessive sometimes to the point of obnoxiousness in his adherence to the traditional values of his society, and who thinks that regardless of the significance of the Week of Peace, a man ought not stop beating his wife halfway through the act. By assigning the traits of excess and uncompromise to the protagonist of the novel, Achebe implies that Okonkwo's inflexible adherence to what he perceives to be the values of his society without any real analysis, questioning, brings about his own destruction in the end and, by extension, the destruction or falling apart of the entire clan. . . .

For, to be sure, although Achebe has said that Africa had a well-developed and dignified culture long before the Europeans imposed upon it an alien way of life, he has also stated that

> We cannot pretend that our past was one long techni-color idyll. We have to admit that like other people's past ours had its good and bad sides.

Hence, it seems clear that in looking back toward the dissolution of Ibo society and its values in *Things Fall Apart*, Achebe demonstrates through excessive actions and uncompromising stances of Okonkwo that the disintegration of the Umuofian clan was merely hastened, not entirely caused by European intervention. . . .

Achebe Analyzes Ibo and European Values

In a recent interview when speaking of Okonkwo's character in general and his killing of Ikemefuna in particular, Achebe commented upon the protagonist's literalism thus:

> Okonkwo is a single-minded person who accepts what he feels as the norms of his community and acts in a kind of literal-minded way. He is not going to be swayed by any other considerations other than those he understands his community stands for. And he is right. But his community is always ready at the moment of crisis to bend a little, whereas someone like Okonkwo, who is literal-minded, will not bend to the community. For example, when he kills Ike-

mefuna, his community condemns the act. But for Okonkwo, somebody has to kill him because the society *says* he should be killed.

Here, in this analysis of Okonkwo's literal-mindedness, Achebe asserts that all societies have their negative and positive qualities, and the unthinking people of these societies, who make no distinction between the bad and the good, can do irreparable harm to their communities. The ritualistic killing of Ikemefuna and the abandonment of the twins are two of these negative acts, both mandatory in the Ibo system, yet both irrational and inhumane. However, Okonkwo never once questions the ethics of either practice. Societies themselves, Achebe implies, sometimes plant the seeds that can hasten their own disintegration, and the Ibo society is no exception. And such negative seeds placed into the hands of a literal-minded man like Okonkwo, who takes it upon himself to champion *all* the values of Ibo tribal life without careful analysis or questions, can indeed become very destructive to the fabric of society.

In holding the defects of the Ibo value system up to analysis, Achebe does not overlook the numerous shortcomings of the European value system exported to Nigeria by the British and imposed upon the indigenous people. Although some critics hold that Achebe in the manner of a historian makes no value judgment upon either social system or dogmatic assertion upon which system is better or worse, the European system does come in for a sounder thrashing than the Ibo system, despite the fact that Achebe is not as extreme as other African writers in his analysis. . . .

Missionaries Appeal to Outcasts

During the period of Okonkwo's exile, Christian missionaries and British government officials arrive in the Umuofian village. With their guile, self-righteousness, and feelings of superiority, they first appeal to the outcasts or nonconformists of

Some of the impact of the mix of colonial and indigenous cultures can be seen in this Igbo New Year Festival in Nigeria. © Val and Alan Wilkinson/Eye Ubiquitous/Alamy.

Ibo society. One of these nonconformists is Okonkwo's oldest son, Nwoye, who has become disturbed about the senseless killing of his adopted brother, Ikemefuna, and about the tribal custom of abandoning new-born twins to die in the Evil Forest. . . .

Some critics have commented upon the objective manner in which Achebe presents the methods and techniques of the white missionaries and the British government officials. Another, in a similar vein, has noted the balanced treatment given to both the strengths and defects of the African and European value systems. Still another has gone so far as to assert that Achebe sees the new dispensation as something desirable. . . .

However, upon a careful reading of the narrative, it becomes clear that Achebe is demonstrating how the two white missionaries used different means to achieve the same ends; that is, to subvert the values of the indigenous culture. Realizing that a frontal attack on the religion of the clan will not succeed, Mr. Brown chooses instead to build a school in which to indoctrinate the natives with European values.

The missionaries and British government officials could not have succeeded had not some of the indigenous people cooperated with their tactics. Some of the latter, for example, were given "lucrative" positions in the government, where they cooperated in oppressing their own people. . . .

Seeing with the Lens of the Colonizers

When the forces of history all converge in chapter twenty-five of the novel, Achebe puts the reader into the mind of the white District Commissioner, the archetype of the European administrator, who becomes an instant "expert" on Africa. Viewing the mores of Ibo society from a narrow perspective, the commissioner demonstrates his ethnocentric bias in his inability to understand the human dimensions of Okonkwo's fate and in his use of the phrase "Primitive Tribes" in the title of his proposed book about African history. For example, when Okonkwo's body is found hanging from a tree, Obierika and members of the clan refuse to bury him in keeping with tribal custom. Rather, Obierika requests the District Commissioner to ask his men to perform the burial rites, since they are strangers. Lacking the capacity to perceive the significance and human dimensions of Okonkwo's tragedy, the commissioner does order his chief messenger to take down Okonkwo's body "and bring it and all these people to the court." However, because he sees everything from a narrow western perspective, the District Commissioner, who is a symbol of tribal disintegration and administrative oppression, views Okonkwo's death only as an opportunity to give a pointless lesson on European etiquette:

> In the many years in which he had toiled to bring civilization to different parts of Africa he had learned a number of things. One of them was that a District Commissioner must never attend to details as cutting a hanged man from the

tree. Such attention would give the natives a poor opinion of him. In the book which he planned to write he would stress that point.

Hence, Okonkwo's death and the District Commissioner's insensitive attitude toward the African way of life intensify the reader's awareness of the demoralizing effects that colonialism wreaked upon the indigenous people of Nigeria. This same insensitivity and ethnocentrism are again displayed when the commissioner tells of his intention to write only one paragraph about Okonkwo's death and, by extension, the dying of the Ibo way of life in his proposed book about the African experience, *The Pacification of the Primitive Tribes of the Lower Niger.*

The irony in the commissioner's statement is too obvious for the reader to ignore. Not only does the commissioner plan to de-emphasize the death of Ibo culture by writing only one paragraph about Okonkwo's death, but also the Umuofian clansmen stood by and allowed that history to be diminished without putting up any real resistance. Only Okonkwo escapes the final irony of the situation through taking his own life, an act especially horrible within the African context.

In summary, Chinua Achebe's novel, *Things Fall Apart*, is an extremely well-written work demonstrating the author's narrative skill and technique. The work details the conflict in values between the old order represented by Okonkwo and his clan, and the values of the new order represented by Christianity and British colonialism. In the novel, the Ibos are initially pictured as deriving peace and contentment from rural life and from the unity of the Umuofian clan before the arrival of the Europeans. After the latter's advent, the peace and unity of the clan are disturbed as a result of the imported ideas forced upon them by the British missionaries and government officials. Then the clan falls apart in spite of Okonkwo's final abortive attempt to stem the tide, and the new order represented by the white man's Christianity and way of life seems to triumph.

Okonkwo's Tragedy Is Not Due to Colonialism

Umelo Ojinmah

Umelo Ojinmah heads the Department of English at Nasarawa State University in Keffi, Nigeria. He is the author of Witi Ihimaera: A Changing Vision, *a critical study of the work of the renowned New Zealand author Witi Ihimaera.*

In the following selection, Ojinmah takes exception to the assumption that Okonkwo is a victim of colonialism and its purveyors. He proposes that Okonkwo abused the power and responsibility he had earned within the Igbo culture and paid the price for his own excesses. Ojinmah states that Okonkwo was unable to integrate the male and female attributes valued by his society, and he interpreted their traditions and practices too strictly. By deviating from his society's norms, Okonkwo had already manifested the excesses that led to his tragedy before he came in contact with any Europeans.

Realistic and enlightening as Achebe's portrayal of his society is, his writing is above all else a thematic exploration of the responsibility power imposes on those who exercise it, and of the consequences of its abuse. Achebe creates a cohesive society in *Things Fall Apart* [as critic G.D. Killam writes], "with a stable system of values, with precedents of long-standing acceptance, supported by an oral tradition expressed often in proverbial fashion." This is a society that values masculinity, and measures success [as Kofi Awoonor writes,] "in terms of a full barn, a big household of wives and children, a revered position in the councils of elders, titles, and respect

due to his position. . . . Okonkwo epitomises his society, reflecting as he does its values: 'The Igbo, like most African
peoples, place great store on the manly virtues as depicted by
the wrestling matches and the continuous warring between
the various clans.'" Achebe's characterisation of Okonkwo accords with Awoonor's observation; and G.D. Killam puts it
most succinctly: "At the centre of the community is Okonkwo,
a character of intense individuality, yet one in whom the values most admired by Ibo peoples are consolidated." Illustrat-
ing further, and analysing Okonkwo's traits both as an individual, and as an embodiment of the values of his society,
Killam says:

Okonkwo was 'one of the greatest men of his time', the embodiment of Ibo values, the man who better than most
symbolized his race . . . [and] the premium which is placed
on wealth, courage and valour among the Ibo people.
'Okonkwo was clearly cut out for great things' but he had
earned his reputation, as a wrestler (he brought fame to
himself and his village); as a warrior (he had taken the ap-
proved symbols of his prowess, the heads of five victims by
the time he was twenty-one years old); as a man who had
achieved personal wealth symbolized by his two barns full of
yams, his three wives and, of great importance, the two titles
he had taken, titles which can only be acquired when wealth
has been achieved and quality proven.

[Literary critic] Eustace Palmer, making basically the same
points as Killam, explores the negativism of the society's values:

Okonkwo is what his society has made him, for his most
conspicuous qualities are a response to the demands of his
society. If he is plagued by fear of failure and of weakness it
is because his society puts such premium on success; if he is
obsessed with status it is because his society is preoccupied
with rank and prestige; if he is always itching to demonstrate his prowess in war it is because his society reveres

bravery and courage, and measures success by the number of human heads a man has won; if he is contemptuous of weaker men it is because his society has conditioned him into despising cowards. Okonkwo is the personification of his society's values, and is determined to succeed in this rat-race.

Okonkwo Fails to Achieve Balance

Critics such as Killam, Palmer, [Arthur] Ravenscroft and Awoonor, among others, all agree that Okonkwo incorporates the virtues of his culture as well as its excesses. Awoonor writes that: "Okonkwo ... embodies all the virtues and excesses of this society. He is a wrestler, a leader, an intrepid farmer, a man of wealth, unyielding in the pursuit of the ways of his fathers. . . . Around Okonkwo is heard the rhythmic beats of Umuofia's heart." But Achebe's characterisation of the society highlights the existence of a balance of values. This is maintained by the integration of the male and aggressive qualities of the society with the female and protective qualities which some of Okonkwo's actions do not reflect. . . . It is on account of Okonkwo's refusal to acknowledge this fundamental concept in his society's world- view that, I believe, he parts ways with his society; and this mostly accounts for his tragedy. Most critics of Achebe's *Things Fall Apart*, particularly Killam, believe that Okonkwo is primarily a victim of the undermining of his culture by the colonisers. However, Achebe's characterisation of Okonkwo indicates that the colonial factor is a catalyst, for Okonkwo's excesses are entirely his own responsibility. . . . These excesses are inherent, having manifested themselves time and again before he ever comes into contact with any European. For as Ravenscroft notes:

> Achebe implies throughout that Okonkwo is no mere automative victim of a social setting which encourages the qualities he has cultivated. He does have the power of choice; men as highly regarded as he for courage and strength of character are shown not to have expunged gentleness from

their hearts. Umuofia may place less value on these gentler virtues but does acknowledge and provide for them.

This flexibility of the society contrasts markedly with Okonkwo's single-mindedness. . . .

However, Achebe indicates how Okonkwo's inherent fear of being like his father, of being thought weak and effeminate, leads him to excesses, even to killing Ikemefuna, who has become like a son to him. Many critics, among them Awoonor, trace Okonkwo's final tragedy to this singular act; an act which Obierika prophetically says is "the kind of action for which the [earth] goddess wipes out whole families." . . .

Okonkwo is also shown to be at variance with societal norms in another aspect. Achebe acknowledges that members of Igbo society are traditionally acquisitive and materialistic, but have a spirituality which helps keep the materialism in check:

> Anyone who has given any thought to our society must be concerned by the brazen materialism one sees around. I have heard people blame it on Europe. That is utter rubbish. In fact the Nigerian society I know best—the Ibo society— has always been materialistic. This may sound strange because Ibo life had at the same time a strong spiritual dimension—controlled by gods, ancestors, personal spirits or *chi*, and magic. The success of the culture was the balance between the two, the material and the spiritual.

He goes on further to say: "Today we have kept the materialism and thrown away the spirituality which should keep it in check." Though Okonkwo's "wealth meant the strength of [his] arm" he is however, portrayed as ignoring this spirituality while single-mindedly embracing the materialism.

Okonkwo's Temper Is a Flaw

Added to the above failing, from the traditional society's point of view, Achebe describes Okonkwo's short temper and heavy-handedness, both with outsiders and with members of his household, as constituting grounds for reproach:

> When he walked, his heels hardly touched the ground and he seemed to walk on springs, as if he was going to pounce on somebody. And he did pounce on people quite often. He had a slight stammer and whenever he was angry and could not get his words out quickly enough, he used his fist.... Okonkwo ruled his household with a heavy hand. His wives, especially the youngest, lived in perpetual fear of his fiery temper, and so did his little children.

His inability to control his temper leads him time and again to transgress against the earth goddess, laying a foundation for societal sanction and the explication of the proverb of *nza* the little bird. G.D. Killam has noted that Achebe understates issues, preferring to express more through suggestiveness: "His typical method is based on allusion and implication which leaves much unsaid and thus his writing achieves a suggestiveness which communicates far more than he might achieve in long passages of explicit description." This leads, often, to the apprehension of the symbolic nature of some of Okonkwo's actions, and the society's response to them, only in retrospect.

Achebe characterises Okonkwo as intrepid and aggressive, both in war and on issues of concern to his clan. When one considers this, his high-handedness with members of his immediate family, especially with Nwoye and his younger wives, becomes irrationality bordering on an inability to know when and where to draw the line in exhibiting his manliness. ...

Singled Out for Destruction

The effect of [Okonkwo's] stifling of his emotions was that "people said he had no respect for the gods of the clan. His enemies said his good fortune had gone to his head. They called him the little bird *nza* who so far forgot himself after a heavy meal that he challenged his *chi.*" Kofi Awoonor establishes the link between Okonkwo's arrogance, his tendency to overreach himself, and his abuse of power and his final tragedy by extending Achebe's imagery of 'the little bird *nza*', and "the great wrestler who, after having defeated all men, went into the spirit world and was confronted with a small wiry spirit who smashed him on the stony earth." He further suggests "that perhaps by the very nature of his character, Okonkwo was trying to overreach himself in the public display that accompanies the firing of cannons and guns to salute the dead. So at the height of his achievements and on the verge of achieving greater glories, the gods singled him out for humiliation and destruction."

If Awoonor's reading of Okonkwo's tragedy, that he was singled out for destruction by the gods, is correct, Achebe suggests that his fate is consistent with his calling as a warrior, but most especially it reinforces the traditional belief that the tribal gods are efficacious. Achebe believes that the dawn of colonialism rendered Okonkwo's type functionally redundant. It was therefore judicious and necessary that the gods, in performing their traditional function of protecting the clan, and seeing the old warrior who now constituted a time-bomb whose explosion would annihilate the whole clan as exemplified by the story of Abame, should defuse him the way they did. Achebe notes Okonkwo's deviation from the traditional norm of concert, particularly on decisions about whether or not to go to war which would affect the whole clan: "If Umuofia decided to go to war, all would be well. But if they chose to be cowards he would go out and avenge himself . . . If they listen to [Egonwanne] I shall leave them and plan my own revenge. . . . I shall fight alone if I choose."

Some critics have noted that Okonkwo commits suicide because he could not face the prospect of seeing the tribe disintegrate under the impact of colonialism, and particularly because he felt that the clan has lost the will to fight like their ancestors: "Okonkwo was deeply grieved. And it was not just a

personal grief. He mourned for the clan, which he saw breaking up and falling apart, and he mourned for the warlike men
of Umuofia, who had so unaccountably become soft like
women." But Achebe sees his tragedy as essentially that of
someone whose parochialism blinded him to a complete
awareness of the dynamic functioning of his society's response:
"Life just has to go on and if you refuse to accept changes,
then tragic though it may be, you are swept aside." The
society's ability to adapt to any situation, which [David] Carroll has already noted, is a survival mechanism appropriate to
the new threat. The clan's action, of choosing not to fight a
war they knew they could not win, was consistent with the
wisdom of their ancestors contained in the Igbo adage which
states that: "The man who cannot discern his superior is im-
mature". Achebe's remark that Okonkwo was swept aside because he refused to accept change accords with the theme of
this analysis, that in certain ways he was not representative of
his society. While he embodies the acquisitiveness of his society, its materialism, and its love of manliness, Okonkwo per-
sistently shows an aversion to the other 'female' side on which
the society's survival depends, and it is this that leads to his
tragedy. In Achebe's view, Okonkwo's established deviation
from his society, and the fact that most of his excesses were
already manifest before he ever comes into contact with any
European, indicate abuse of both power and responsibility.

The White Man Redeemed Igbo Society

Romanus Okey Muoneke

*Romanus Okey Muoneke is a member of the English Depart-
ment at the University of St. Thomas in Houston, Texas. He
earned a BA from the University of Nigeria and a PhD in English from the University of Houston. He has taught in Nigeria,
Ireland, and the United States.*

*In the following selection, Muoneke argues that the advent of the
white colonizers actually redeemed Igbo society, which was in the
process of disintegrating as times changed. Brutal and insensitive
practices of the society, and its focus on strength and masculinity,
were countered by the new government and the introduction of
Christianity. In spite of its repressive tactics, Muoneke states, the
colonial government brought courts of law, which granted equal
treatment to all and economic opportunities via trade for its traditional goods. Muoneke concludes that the Igbo were redeemed
by accommodating and compromising with the colonizers.*

Paradoxically, the coming of the white man to Umuofia has
a positive value, which itself is redemptive. . . . Achebe
subscribes to the Yeatsian theory [of Irish poet W.B. Yeats] of
the inevitability of change in the history of any civilization.
Things Fall Apart deals with a crucial period in the history of
Umuofia when the old civilization approaches the brink of
disintegration. Obierika rightly identifies the major source of
this disintegration as the white man: "The white man is very
clever. He came quietly and peaceably with his religion. We
were amused at his foolishness and allowed him to stay. Now

Romanus Okey Muoneke, "Chapter Three: Redemption: *Things Fall Apart*," in *Art, Re-
bellion and Redemption: A Reading of the Novels of Chinua Achebe*, New York, NY:
Peter Lang, 1994, pp. 100–117. Copyright © 1994 Peter Lang Publishing, Inc., New
York. All rights reserved. Reproduced by permission.

he has won our brothers, and our clan can no longer act like one. He has put a knife on the things that held us together and we have fallen apart." But the coming of the white man is an historical imperative, an event Umuofia could not countermand. Umuofia had reached a point where, in Yeats's words, "the centre cannot hold." Like a blighted tree, Umuofia, already fractured by internal flaws, stood tottering at the mercy of any storm. Once threatened by the white man's government and religion, it succumbed.

Yet, the white man's mission was ultimately redemptive. Umuofia was already sick and had to be "doctored." Apart from the many acts of brutality the society embraced, like abandoning twins in the forests, mutilating *ogbanje* children after death, abandoning victims of swelling sickness to die in the forest, the society of Umuofia is shown to have failed to extend protection to the weak, the poor, women, and the outcasts (*osu*). Monstrous injunctions of the gods were promptly executed without human consideration, and contravention of certain laws drew terrible penalties. Okonkwo's seven years of exile for the accidental shooting of his friend's son is a typical example of such harsh penalties. In addition to the sentence of exile, his houses were set ablaze, his barns destroyed, and his animals killed by the men of Umuofia who stormed his compound, dressed like warriors. Obierika, one of the participants in this exercise, was later moved to question traditional justice:

> Obierika was a man who thought about things. When the will of the goddess had been done, he sat down in his *obi* and mourned his friend's calamity. Why should a man suffer so grievously for an offense he had committed inadvertently? But although he thought for a long time he found no answer. He was merely led to greater complexities. He remembered his wife's twin children, whom he had thrown away. What crime had they committed?

Obierika acts as Achebe's mouthpiece in this analysis. The passage is a direct commentary on society's inhumanity. This inhuman practice places Umuofia in a morally vulnerable position, which the missionaries could readily exploit upon their arrival.

Nwoye Questions Igbo Traditions

Apart from Obierika, Nwoye also questioned his society's traditional practices. He was never impressed by the clan's celebration of strength and masculinity. His taste was a far cry from that of his father who prepared him for a "manly" life by telling him stories of violence and bloodshed. But Nwoye preferred "women stories." Greatly disturbed by the death of his "brother" and mentor Ikemefuna, a death for which he held his father suspect, and worried about the clan's insensitive and chilling practice in connection with the abandoned twins he had chanced upon crying in the thick forest, Nwoye became alienated from his people. The coming of Ikemefuna had significantly boosted his morale and given him fulfillment. It had made him "feel grown up" and "seemed to have kindled a new fire" in him. When he sensed that Ikemefuna had been killed, "something seemed to give way inside him, like the snapping of a tightening bow." The death of Ikemefuna signaled his final break with the traditional Umuofia society. Henceforth, he became a quiet rebel against the traditional norms. It also explains his rejection of Okonkwo, who epitomized the cruelty in these norms. The coming of the Christians to Mbanta led him to discover in them what he had lost in the deceased Ikemefuma, a brotherhood. His decision to become an early convert is based upon "natural law" and prefigures his recognition of a higher moral ethos.

Christianity Redeems Some Igbos

Christianity was for Nwoye a redemptive event. Redemption is Christianity's fundamental mission. Christ is the symbol of redemption, especially as he fulfills the prophecy of Isaiah: "*to*

Some of the benefits of colonial tools and science can be seen in this picture of volunteers of Igbo descent creating egg-shaped molds of clay to build mud huts at the Igbo village at the Frontier Culture Museum in Staunton, Virginia, in 2009. AP Images.

bring the good news to the afflicted. / He has sent me to pro-claim liberty to captives, / sight to the blind, / to let the op-pressed go free" (Luke 4:18–19; Is 61:1–2). Achebe sees Christianity as largely contributing to the destruction of the traditional system, but also as redeeming the victims of the old system. The conversion of Nwoye to Christianity is explained by its synaesthesia:

> It was not the mad logic of the Trinity that captivated him. He did not understand it. It was the poetry of the new religion, something felt in the marrow. The hymn about brothers who sat in darkness and in fear seemed to answer a vague and persistent question that haunted his young soul— the question of the twins crying in the bush and the question of Ikemefuna who was killed. He felt a relief within as the hymn poured into his parched soul. The words of the hymn were like the drops of frozen rain melting on the dry palate of the panting earth.

Life, Hope, and New Values

In Nwoye, the convert, the life of cruelty and insensitivity, represented with images of barrenness, gave way to a new life of poetry and brotherhood, represented with images of rain. Christianity, therefore, gives life and hope. For Okonkwo, Christianity was "womanish" because it signifies those values which he despised—love, affection, gentleness, and mercy. But it is precisely these values for which Nwoye had yearned and now found in Christianity. Many others in Umuofia felt as Nwoye and saw Christianity as a refuge for the oppressed and the underdogs: the so-called *efulefu* or "worthless, empty men"; the *osu* or outcasts who were virtually ostracized from society which would not allow them to marry nor permit them be married to free-borns; parents of twins; and those held in contempt because they had taken no titles.

The missionaries, themselves, included people who exhibited exemplary qualities. An example is Mr. Brown who displayed the vitality of Christian faith in his reverence for his fellow man. He educated the people and cared for their welfare. His willingness to listen to the people and learn from them about their own culture enabled him to carry out his mission in a very hospitable manner. He not only cared for the people's spiritual welfare by building new churches, he also cared for their material progress; hence, he built a school and a hospital. Consequently, "his mission grew from strength to strength."

Colonizers Make Positive Contribution

The colonial administration also made a positive contribution, despite the oppression it represented. The aim of the colonial government, as stated by the District Commissioner, was to grant protection to all the people, irrespective of age or rank, and to promote peace and justice. Addressing the six elders of Umuofia who had been arrested as a result of the violence against Christians before humiliating them, he said: "We have brought a peaceful administration to you and your people so that you may be happy. If any man ill-treats you we shall come to your rescue. But we will not allow you to ill-treat others. We have a court of law where we judge cases and administer justice just as it is done in my own country under a great queen." The new administration, therefore, aimed to introduce a system which would grant equal treatment to all and curb the excesses based on superstition, fear, and brutality. In carrying out its aims, the administration may have faltered, . . . yet it is significant that its primary purpose was the institution of law and order and fair treatment to all. The ultimate beneficiaries of the new system would be those who felt unfairly treated in the tribal system. Another redemptive aspect of the new administration proved to be the material benefits it introduced into Umuofia for which it won the loyalty of many men and women: "The white man had indeed brought a lunatic religion, but he had also brought a trading store and for the first time palm-oil and kernel became things of great price, and much money flowed in Umuofia." The people enjoyed the social uplift resulting from the economic progress introduced by the colonial administration. This partly explains why they did not feel "as strongly as Okonkwo about the new dispensation," and also why it proved difficult for Okonkwo to mobilize them to fight the white man. . . .

Redemption Requires Accepting Change

Things Fall Apart deals with the twilight of an integrated, though fragmented ("cracked" to use Yeats's term), African world at the moment of its confrontation with the European world. It also dramatizes conflicts (personal and cultural) resulting from this confrontation. The tragic nature of the confrontation is signified in the actions of those who, blind to the inevitability of change and the immense power of the white man, resist with violence. Achebe shows in this novel that in such a situation, redemption lies in accommodation and compromise, flexibility and balance. Hence, while men of action like Okonkwo perish in their narrowness of vision and blind resistance, more flexible and accommodating men like Obierika survive.

It is possible to outline Achebe's intent concerning those internal fractures that caused the Igbo culture to implode, as it were, in the face of the invasion of Western culture. In essence, it is foreshadowed in the deteriorating relationship between the members of the male line of Okonkwo's family. Each breaks from the other. There is, in fact, no personal or spiritual relationship from one son to the other. We detect only a biological relationship through the physical mother. There is a total absence of a cultural mother. . . .

It is to the credit of Achebe's literary genius that we are given a glimpse of the future generation. Okonkwo has two sons: the first is his "spiritual" son, Ikemefuna; the other is the son of his loins, Nwoye. Clearly, the future was to have two parts: those who would follow the Igbo tradition, and those who would be absorbed into the West.

Three Distinct Endings Present a Layered Approach to the Colonized Experience

Richard Begam

Richard Begam is a professor of English at the University of Wisconsin–Madison. His literary criticism has been widely published in academic journals and books.

In the following selection, Begam proposes that Things Fall Apart *includes three separate endings: one focused on Okonkwo's killing of the messenger and subsequent suicide, a second from the viewpoint of the British colonizers in their unfeeling management of Okonkwo's suicide, and the third actually taking place in the novel that Achebe wrote after* Things Fall Apart, *titled* No Longer at Ease. *In that ending, Chinua Achebe portrays Okonkwo's grandson as acknowledging that the tragedy of the past is also his own tragedy. Begam asserts that each ending represents a version of the truth.*

In what follows, I will argue that *Things Fall Apart* resists the idea of a single or simple resolution by providing three distinct endings, three different ways of reading the events that conclude the novel. At the same time, I will relate these endings to three different conceptions of history, especially as it is produced within a postcolonial context. First, Achebe writes a form of nationalist history. Here the interest is essentially reconstructive and centers on recovering an Igbo past that has been neglected or suppressed by historians who would not or could not write from an African perspective. As Achebe observed in 1964, four years after Nigerian independence: "His-

Richard Begam, "Achebe's Sense of an Ending: History and Tragedy in *Things Fall Apart*," *Studies in the Novel*, vol. XXIX, no. 3, Fall 1997, pp. 396–411. Copyright © 1997 by the University of North Texas. Reproduced by permission.

torians everywhere are re-writing the stories of the new nations—replacing short, garbled, despised history with a more sympathetic account." Nationalist history tends to emphasize what other histories have either glossed over or flatly denied—namely that "African people did not hear of culture for the first time from Europeans; that their societies were not mindless but frequently had a philosophy of great depth and value and beauty, that they had poetry and, above all, they had dignity." Second, Achebe writes a form of adversarial history. Here the emphasis falls not on the reconstruction of an authentic past that has been lost, but on the deconstruction of a counterfeit past that has been imposed. Adversarial history enables Achebe to write against what he himself has called "colonialist" discourse, against the attitudes and assumptions, the language and rhetoric that characterized British colonial rule in Nigeria. Third, Achebe writes a form of metahistory. This kind of history calls attention to itself as a piece of writing, a narrative construction that depends on principles of selection (what material will be included?), emphasis (what importance will be attached to it?) and shaping (how will it be organized and arranged?). . . .

Okonkwo's Tragedy Mirrors the Igbos' Fate

The first of the novel's three endings centers on Okonkwo's killing of the messenger, his failed attempt to rouse his people to action, and his subsequent suicide. This ending presents the events of the novel largely from an African perspective, equating Okonkwo's demise with the collapse of Igbo culture. The idea that Okonkwo is a great man whose destiny is linked with that of his people is immediately established in the novel's celebrated opening:

> Okonkwo was well known throughout the nine villages and even beyond. His fame rested on solid personal achievements. As a young man of eighteen he had brought honor to his village by throwing Amalinze the Cat. Amalinze was

the great wrestler who for seven years was unbeaten, from Umuofia to Mbano. He was called the Cat because his back would never touch the earth. It was this man that Okonkwo threw in a fight which the old men agreed was one of the fiercest since the founder of their town engaged a spirit of the wild for seven days and seven nights.

In this passage history recedes into myth, as the narrator presents the seven-year reign of Amalinze and the seven-day struggle of the founder of the village in epic terms. . . . The passage also serves both to connect Okonkwo with the beginnings of Umuofia (through his wrestling exploits he is compared with the village's symbolic progenitor) and to look forward to his own and his people's end (the "spirit of the wild," representing Nature, will be replaced by the more powerful alien force of British imperialism.) In a few deft strokes, Achebe illustrates how Okonkwo has come to personify the destiny of his community, extending from its earliest origins to its final destruction.

The larger effect of Achebe's opening is to establish Okonkwo as a particular kind of tragic protagonist: the great warrior who carries with him the fate of his people. Seen from the standpoint of the first ending, he is, as [literary critic] Michael Valdez Moses has argued, a Homeric hero cast in a distinctly Achillean mold. . . .

Okonkwo is, in other words, identified with his community to the extent that it esteems the martial [warlike] ethos he embodies, and while his village certainly does more than make war, it especially prizes those men who win distinction on the battlefield. . . .

Okonkwo Is a Flawed Hero

This is not to say, however, that Okonkwo epitomizes all the virtues of Igbo culture, or that he is himself without fault. On the contrary, Achebe himself understands that, within an Aristotelian framework, his hero is necessarily a flawed character, guilty of errors in judgement—guilty, to use the Greek term, of *hamartia* [transgression]. . . . Obviously Okonkwo is "larger than life" ("He was tall and huge, and his bushy eyebrows and wide nose gave him a very severe look") yet his epic proportions carry a figurative as well as a literal significance: they indicate the difficulty he experiences fitting within the boundaries of any social order. . . . Nevertheless, if we are to appreciate the tragedy of the first ending—something that Achebe clearly intends—then we must recognize that Okonkwo's faults are essentially virtues carried to an extreme, and that while he is obviously not perfect, he nevertheless represents some of the best qualities of his culture. As Obierika remarks near the novel's end, "That man was one of the greatest men in Umuofia."

Killing of Messenger Symbolic of Igbo Conflict

The crisis of the novel comes in the penultimate chapter when an impudent messenger, sent by the colonial authorities, orders a tribal meeting to disband. Okonkwo the warrior is moved to action:

> In a flash Okonkwo drew his machete. The messenger crouched to avoid the blow. It was useless. Okonkwo's machete descended twice and the man's head lay beside his uniformed body.
>
> The waiting backcloth jumped into tumultuous life and the meeting was stopped. Okonkwo stood looking at the dead man. He knew that Umuofia would not go to war. He knew because they had let the other messengers escape. They had broken into tumult instead of action. He discerned fright in that tumult. He heard voices asking: "Why did he do it?"
>
> He wiped his machete on the sand and went away.

The scene is presented with a devastating simplicity. From the perspective of the first ending, the people of Umuofia have deserted Okonkwo and in the process betrayed themselves, but the wiping of the machete is the only eloquence he permits himself. It is an ordinary and everyday gesture, yet in the present context it acquires special significance: Okonkwo remains true to the martial ethos that his people have abandoned, here represented by the warrior's care of his weapon; at the same time, he symbolically dissolves his connection with his people, wiping away the blood bond that has joined them. This gesture is especially resonant because, as critics have pointed out, in killing the messenger he is shedding the blood of a fellow Igbo.

Suicide Foreshadows Cultural Destruction

The suicide that follows is itself a profound violation of Igbo law, which strictly prohibits acts of self-destruction. . . . Hence, understood within the terms of the novel's first ending, Okonkwo's suicide is the logical and necessary consequence of an idealistic and absolutist position. Both nationalist history and heroic tragedy demand that he remain unyielding and that the Igbos honor their cultural heritage by refusing assimilation. Even in this final gesture, then, Okonkwo functions as the true representative of his people. For, as he sees it, Igbo culture has willingly succumbed to its own annihilation, committing what is a form of collective suicide by submitting to the British. In taking his own life, Okonkwo has simply preceded his people in their communal destruction. Once again he has led the way. . . .

The Viewpoint of the Colonizers

The novel's second ending, which I associate with adversarial history, views events from the heavily ironized perspective of the District Commissioner. Igbo culture is now presented not from the inside as vital and autonomous, but from the outside as an object of anthropological curiosity, and its collapse is understood not as an African tragedy but as a European triumph. As the final scene of the novel unfolds, the Igbos take the District Commissioner to the place where the suicide was committed:

> Then they came to the tree from which Okonkwo's body was dangling, and they stopped dead.
>
> "Perhaps your men can help us bring him down and bury him," said Obeirika. "We have sent for strangers from another village to do it for us, but they may be a long time coming."
>
> The District Commissioner changed instantaneously. The resolute administrator in him gave way to the student of primitive customs.
>
> "Why can't you take him down yourselves?" he asked.
>
> "It is against our custom," said one of the men. "It is an abomination for a man to take his own life."

What is particularly noteworthy in this episode is the way the District Commissioner effortlessly shifts from the "resolute administrator" to the "student of primitive customs." . . . Thus, those who wrote historical and anthropological accounts of the Igbos were typically either representatives of the British government or their semi-official guests, and the colonial administration not only helped to enable such research by "opening up" various regions, but also relied upon it in determining local policy. . . . By way of illustration we might consider how the scene with the District Commissioner continues:

> "Take down the body," the Commissioner ordered his chief messenger, "and bring it and all these people to the court."
>
> "Yes, sah," the messenger said, saluting.
>
> The Commissioner went away, taking three or four of the soldiers with him. In the many years in which he had toiled to bring civilization to different parts of Africa he had

learned a number of things. One of them was that a District Commissioner must never attend to such undignified details as cutting a hanged man from the tree. Such attention would give the natives a poor opinion of him. In the book which he planned to write he would stress that point. . . .

The Illusion of Understanding

What the District Commissioner ultimately achieves is not genuine understanding but the illusion of understanding that comes with the power to control:

> Every day brought him some new material. The story of this man who had killed a messenger and hanged himself would make interesting reading. One could almost write a whole chapter on him. Perhaps not a whole chapter but a reasonable paragraph, at any rate. There was so much else to include, and one must be firm in cutting out details. He had already chosen the title of the book, after much thought: *The Pacification of the Primitive Tribes of the Lower Niger.*

With these words, *Things Fall Apart* completes its passage from the heroic tragedy of the first ending to the biting irony of the second ending. . . . By ironically undermining the perspective of the District Commissioner, by exposing the latter's personal ignorance (not a "whole chapter" but a "reasonable paragraph") and political interests (the "pacification" of the Lower Niger), Achebe seeks to confront and finally to discredit the entire discourse of colonialism, those quasi-historical, quasi-anthropological writings that have treated Africa as nothing more than—again I quote Achebe—"a foil to Europe, a place of negations." . . .

All Three Endings Reflect Cultural Loss

What I shall identify as the third ending is located in *No Longer At Ease*, the sequel to *Things Fall Apart*. No doubt, the assertion that one text contains the ending of another will immediately strike some readers as dubious. Such a claim begins to gain credibility, however, when we remember that Achebe originally conceived of his two novels as the first and third sections of a single work. ... Both novels tell the story of a representative of the Igbo people who takes a stand on a question of principle and is destroyed in the ensuing collision between African and European values. ...

The point of intersection between the two novels, the scene in which I locate the third ending of *Things Fall Apart*, occurs when Okonkwo's grandson, Obi, a university-educated civil servant, finds himself discussing tragedy with a British colonial officer. Obi advances the opinion—of special interest given the first ending of *Things Fall Apart*—that suicide ruins a tragedy:

> Real tragedy is never resolved. It goes on hopelessly forever. Conventional tragedy is too easy. The hero dies and we feel a purging of the emotions. A real tragedy takes place in a corner, in an untidy spot, to quote W.H. Auden. The rest of the world is unaware of it. Like that man in *A Handful of Dust* who reads Dickens to Mr. Todd. There is no release for him. When the story ends he is still reading. There is no purging of the emotions for us because *we are not there.* ...

Indeed, if Achebe provides us with any controlling point of view, it comes with the third ending, which illustrates the vexed and ambiguous relation in which the postcolonial stands to its own past. For with his remarks on tragedy, Obi is offering a narrative analysis of what is *literally* his own past. In describing a tragedy that ends in suicide, he is describing his grandfather's tragic fall and its significance for Igbo culture after it was lost, after "things fell apart."

What the novel's third ending illustrates, then, is that the boundaries between the "conventional" and the "real," the heroic and the ironic, are not clearly or cleanly drawn. From Obi's perspective—and, for that matter, the reader's—Okonkwo functions both as a literary persona and a living person, an epic hero and an historical anachronism. Yet the novel does not invite us to select one of these alternatives so much as to understand the various, though decidedly distinctive, truths they articulate. In other words, we are not meant to choose from among three possible endings, but to read all of them, as it were, simultaneously and palimpsestically [in layers]. If we are able to do this, we shall see how Achebe's sense of an ending is intimately bound up with his sense of cultural loss; how the tragedy of the past necessarily depends on the perspective of the present; and how history is inevitably written for both the "they who were there" and the "we who are not there."

Social Issues
in Literature

Contemporary
Perspectives
on Colonialism

Foreign Aid Is a Twenty-First-Century Form of Colonialism

John A. Burton

John A. Burton is the chief executive officer of World Land Trust, an international conservation charity that works to preserve biologically important threatened lands.

In the following viewpoint, Burton promotes the concept that relief aid imposes Northern Hemisphere values and aspirations on areas such as Africa, creating a twenty-first-century form of colonialism. Foreign aid destroys traditional cultures and creates dependency. Further, argues Burton, aid absolves the local governments of their responsibilities for their people.

One of the problems that biologists have is reconciling empiricism with the world we live in, and the ethics of modern society. Nowhere is this more apparent than in the sphere of conflict and war. I should make my own position clear. Morally and politically I am a pacifist. However, as a naturalist, I observe animals; and man, as an animal, engages in intraspecific competition, which often culminates in warfare. The disturbing thing about this is that based on all the available evidence, this is the natural state of affairs.

Working on the Causes of Conflict

Long-term peace, in human populations, is abnormal, rather than normal, and has always been so. At low population densities, relative peace is usually established, depending on the obvious factors such as allocation of resources. But as soon as

John A. Burton, "Warfare and Wildlife, and Missionaries," *World Land Trust*, April 12, 2006. Reproduced by permission.

During the famine in Somalia, protesters display signs indicating that they need food but not an occupying force that could subject them to colonial powers. © Bernard Bisson/ Sygma/Corbis.

resources become scarce, and inequalities start to emerge, and populations grow, then warfare, be it tribal or national, starts to become the norm. This is a fact that few politicians seem to recognise, and few aid agencies accept when developing strategies. If warfare and conflict is accepted as being normal behaviour, then it becomes an absolute essential to work on the causes, if one is trying to solve the problems of the results. And this is something I see little or no evidence of aid charities ever even considering. Actually, that is not entirely right, since I did note that Oxfam do have projects relating to land rights in Africa—probably an essential step forward for preventing environmental degradation, and also one that helps prevent conflict.

Northern Hemisphere Values

On the broader issues, while reflecting on the way relief and other forms of aid are delivered, I am increasingly of the opinion that much of the foreign aid, particularly in Africa, is a 21st century form of colonialism, imposing the values and

121

aspirations of the northern hemisphere on the south. There seems to me to be very little difference between modern aid, and the evangelist missionaries of a century ago. Both destroy traditional cultures, both create dependency, both create markets for imported goods. Just as our grandparents felt good when they gave a few shillings to send missionaries to save their souls, too many people give a few pounds to salve their own consciences, without thinking about the long-term consequences.

I am certainly not saying I know the answers, but I do know that most of the aid does not have long term benefits. Even worse, it is often absolving governments of taking responsibility for their own shortcomings. Because, in reality, most African governments could provide far more money than Live Aid and similar charitable activities raise, if only they stopped buying arms from Britain and other rich countries, and they stopped the outflow of capital. Buying cows for African farmers, and digging more wells is a short term solution that will invariably create long term problems. Sending old clothes creates a demand for designer labels, which in turn creates another dependency, as well as exporting capital to the northern hemisphere.

One of the problems concerning aid is that it is extremely difficult to get honest evaluations. All donor agencies, be they government, intergovernmental, or NGOs [nongovernmental organizations] always tend to write up projects as successes. If all the millions of dollars, pounds and euros spent on aid have financed so many successful projects, how come Africa is in such a mess?

The One Laptop per Child Project Is a Form of Colonialism

Stanley Douglas Stych

Stanley Douglas Stych is a writer and blogger who lives in Berkeley, California.

In the following viewpoint, Stych asserts that the One Laptop per Child project is misguided and constitutes colonialism in that it makes assumptions about what a native population needs, rather than seeking their input. He states that the money spent on developing low-cost laptops for children in developing countries would be better used to meet their basic needs such as food, shelter, clean water, sanitation, and immunizations. Stych says it would cost less per child to build libraries and schools where all children would have access to learning tools.

Yes, there's been breaking news on the OLPC [One Laptop per Child] project. Very soon US residents will be able to purchase two of the $100 laptops for only $399 (no, it's not a new Apple product) one for themselves and one for some fortunate child in the developing world. Orders for the laptops have been a little slower than anticipated, so this scheme was implemented to raise money for the project.

Cheap Laptops for Developing Countries

What the heck is the OLPC project? In a nutshell, it's a plan to produce a cheap robust laptop for use under conditions where the infrastructure is less than ideal: the developing world. It has no moving parts, can be read in sunlight, and is

Stanley Douglas Stych, "Colonialism's New Look for the 21st Century: OLPC, One Laptop Per Child," unitedcats.wordpress.com (Doug's Darkworld), September 24, 2007. Reproduced by permission.

powered by a foot pump, solar power, or a pull-string powered charger. A laptop that can be used by children in the developing world for a reasonable cost, ultimately the goal being only $100 per child. It's also waterproof. (After seeing a friend destroy a free laptop with a single drop of coffee, I'd think all laptops would be waterproof, but what do I know?)

OLPC, the organization developing and promoting this project, is a non profit organization. An attempt to bring the modern world to children in the developing world, what could possibly be wrong with helping children?

Children Have More Important Needs

Here's my theory: Whenever someone says something is "for the children," one should immediately narrow one's eyes and focus one's mind, because you've just been alerted that someone is trying to pull a fast one on you. In this case, the immediate question one should ask is, What do children in the developing world need? For starters: 1.5 million children die in the developing world every year due to lack of access to clean water and sanitation. Another 2.2 million die for want of a few dollars worth of immunizations. This is our solution, give 'em $100 laptops?! Think of the creative blog entries! "My little sister died today because we couldn't afford a dollar's worth of medicine, but thank God some rich westerner gave me this laptop so I can blog about it!"

Ah, the humanity. Yes, I am sure that many of the people behind this project are truly trying to do a good thing. I hope. I mean, superficially it does sound like a neat idea, give the poor children of the world a leg up into the information age, how can that be bad? Well, for one thing, as noted above, there are tens of millions of children in the developing world who have far more pressing needs: food, clean water, and shelter. For a second thing, libraries and schools could be built to give poor children far more effective learning resources than just a laptop . . . for *far less* money per child. Hmm, the pro-

Pupils work on their laptops on October 1, 2008, in a rural school in Rincón de Vignoli, some 50 miles north of Montevideo, Uruguay. Uruguay made the first official order of 100,000 laptops from the One Laptop per Child (OLPC) initiative in October 2007. Miguel Rojo/AFP/Getty Images.

ponents of this project don't mention that. Thirdly, these laptops are going to be *sold* to the nations of the developing world . . . for cold hard western cash.

Colonialism in Disguise

In other words, no matter how well intentioned some of the participants may be, this is a project primarily designed to suck $100 per child out of the poorest nations on Earth under the guise of helping them. In the old days this was called colonialism, and many people then also truly thought they were helping the poor Godless natives. Now we call it "helping the children." Nothing has really changed since the day the Dutch "bought" Manhattan for a few trunks full of trade goods; we get their resources for far less than their actual value, and the natives get beads and blankets.

Norfolk Islanders Resist Colonization by Australia

Kathy Marks

Kathy Marks is a journalist and reporter for the U.K. newspaper The Independent *and has published a book titled* Lost Paradise: From Mutiny on the *Bounty* to a Modern-Day Legacy of Sexual Mayhem, *chronicling the sexual abuse trials and aftermath of the mayor of Pitcairn and five other men.*

Norfolk Island is a self-governing territory in the South Pacific where descendants of the renowned mutiny on the English ship known as the Bounty *have lived for generations. In the following selection, Marks reports that the Norfolk Islanders are generally satisfied with their culture and semiautonomous political status. Most are resistant to government interference by Australia. Marks asserts that the Norfolk Islanders see Australia as manipulating the Norfolk government to achieve its own goals.*

To the tourists who alight at Norfolk Island's picturesque airport, this speck of land in the South Pacific seems like paradise. It has beautiful beaches and rolling green hills, but no income tax, no traffic lights, and no mobile phones. The pace of life is so laid-back that the plump Jersey cows have right of way on the roads.

But beneath Norfolk's serene exterior, rebellion is stirring. The island was settled by descendants of the Bounty mutineers in 1856, and has a tradition of resisting political interference. Now it faces a fate that some locals regard as catastrophic: takeover by Australia.

Norfolk, situated 900 miles north-east of Sydney, started life as a British penal colony so brutal that it was known as

Kathy Marks, "21st Century Colonialism: Mutiny on 'Bounty' Island," *The Independent*, June 16, 2006. Reproduced by permission.

Hell in the Pacific. An Australian external territory, the island—five miles long by three miles wide—has governed itself
for 27 years, administering health, welfare, justice and immigration. But with Australia jittery about regional security and
the local economy in the doldrums, the colonial power is preparing to step in.

Canberra is considering two options for Norfolk's future,
both of which would reduce its autonomy. One would consign
it to the status of a shire council. While some islanders wel-
come the prospect of closer integration with Australia, many
fear that it would jeopardise their unique identity.

Just under half of the 1,800-strong population traces its
ancestry back to Pitcairn Island, the South Pacific sanctuary of
Fletcher Christian and his fellow mutineers. The English sail-
ors fled there in 1790 with a group of Polynesian women, after setting their captain, William Bligh, adrift in an open boat
and seizing their ship, the *Bounty*. Their heirs were joined by
three British men—John Buffett, John Evans and George
Nobbs—and the community soon threatened to outgrow tiny
Pitcairn. With the last convicts about to leave for Tasmania,
Queen Victoria offered Norfolk Island to the Pitcairners as a
new home. They decamped en masse, making the 3,700-mile
voyage, although a few homesick families later returned, form-
ing the basis of the modern population on Pitcairn.

While Norfolk Islanders have inter-married with Austra-
lians and New Zealanders, they remain fiercely proud of their
roots. They speak a dialect that blends Tahitian with Old English, and they still cook and fish the Polynesian way. Many
bear their ancestors' surnames; in fact, there are so many
Christians, McCoys, Quintals and so on that the telephone di-
rectory lists certain people by nicknames, such as Lettuce Leaf,
Cane Toad, Tarzan and Smudgie.

It all sounds charming, but the locals fear that the introduction of welfare payments and a new immigration regime
will trigger an influx of Australian "dole bludgers" seeking an

easy life in the sun. At present only people with a job or money to invest are allowed in. The islanders say that their idiosyncratic customs will disappear, and their relaxed way of life will be eroded, if Norfolk becomes just another outpost of Australia. They cherish such liberties as not having to wear seatbelts, and being able to leave their houses unlocked and their car keys in the ignition.

Change is not readily accepted on Norfolk, which has had television and telephones only since the 1980s. Placards proclaiming "Go home Aussie" were posted around the island when an Australian minister visited last year. Some locals are now demanding independence.

That idea seems fanciful, given the size of the place and the decline of the tourism industry, the mainstay of the economy. Norfolk, which was once a popular destination for the "newly-wed and nearly-dead", does not even have a harbour. Supplies, which arrive on a ship from the mainland every few weeks, are ferried ashore on whaleboats.

Some locals, such as Mary Christian-Bailey, whose family owns a tourist apartment complex called Fletcher Christian, smell a hidden agenda in Australia's plans. That agenda is oil, claims Mrs Christian-Bailey, referring to as yet unmined gas hydrates that lie within Norfolk's marine territorial limits. "There is a strong feeling that that is the main reason why Australia would like to take us over," she said.

Mrs Christian-Bailey described the islanders as "extremely peace-loving and polite". But she warned that they might take direct action if they felt backed against a wall by Canberra. "I can't imagine violence, perhaps a little rudeness," she said.

A couple of miles away in the capital, Kingston, the site of imposing stone buildings from the convict era, Geoff Gardner sat fuming in his office. Mr Gardner, the island's Chief Minister for six years, had just been deposed in a coup that he claimed was engineered by Australian "lobbyists". Demoted to Speaker of the nine-member Legislative Assembly, Mr Gardner remains robustly opposed to Australian rule. "This is a place that was given to the people of Pitcairn to inhabit as their own for ever and a day," he said. "They wish to continue to determine their own destiny, and not have it determined by a colonial power wanting to extend its influence."

On the wall behind him was a portrait of the Queen. "God Save the Queen" is still the national anthem on Norfolk. But the island is a strange mix of cultures. Thanksgiving is celebrated, a legacy of the American whalers who settled in the 19th century. The main public holiday is Bounty Day, which commemorates the arrival of the Pitcairners after their epic voyage. Last week Islanders of Pitcairn descent dressed in period costume and congregated on the pier in Kingston to mark the 150th anniversary. In a cemetery overlooking the Pacific, they laid wreaths on their ancestors' graves, before proceeding to a picnic in the grounds of an old convict prison.

The Australian Governor-General, Michael Jeffery, who had flown over for the occasion, complimented them on their "beautiful and bounteous" home. But politics was never far from people's minds. As one islander said: "If they take away our identity, we'll have nothing left."

Not everyone shares those fears. Tom Lloyd, who edited the local newspaper for 40 years and led a "pilgrimage" of Norfolk Islanders back to Pitcairn in 1984, said: "To be frank, I've had difficulty understanding what people are worried about. They can say what they like in Canberra, but we're Norfolk Islanders and we'll always be that, and it's up to us to retain what we believe should be preserved."

Alice Buffett, a highly respected local matriarch and author of a textbook on the Norfolk language, believes the island is incapable of governing itself to the level required. "I disagree with the view that Australia is taking us over," she said, "We've only had self-government since 1979. It's just a matter of putting the genie back in the bottle."

Australia regards Norfolk's system of parliamentary government as excessively complex. Grant Hambling, who is the island's administrator, equivalent to a governor-general, advocates a "more conventional" arrangement. Mr Hambling acknowledged that Norfolk Islanders had "a history of resisting paternalism and imposed change", which some observers linked to their mutinous ancestry, he said. "They don't like Big Brother from Canberra waving a stick. But a lot of the debate is cultural and emotional, and not grounded in sound economics."

Australia says that Norfolk's economy is in such a dire state that the island will go broke within a few months unless drastic remedial action is taken. The locals respond that they have lived through booms and busts before, and some are confident that Norfolk will survive the latest crisis.

Tourism, though, is in decline, partly because of the collapse last year of the local airline. The islanders complain that Australia refused to step in to prop it up.

Meanwhile, the murder in 2002 of a young Australian woman, Janelle Patton, destroyed Norfolk's image as a crime-free haven. It was the first murder on the island in 150 years, and was particularly brutal. A New Zealand man was recently charged, and will face committal proceedings later this year.

Two years after Ms Patton's death, a second murder occurred. Mr Gardner's deputy, Ivens "Toon" Buffett, was shot dead in his office by his son, Leith. Leith Buffett was suffering from a mental illness and is in the psychiatric wing of a Sydney prison.

Many islanders say that Norfolk lost its innocence when Ms Patton, who was a temporary resident, was killed. Now they are fighting to conserve what they have left.

"We don't want government by remote control," said Mrs Christian-Bailey. "When the Pitcairners came here, they believed the land would be theirs to use as they wished, and that they would be allowed to live according to their own laws and customs. It seems they were brought here under false pretences."

French Revisionists Attempted to Defend Colonialism in Africa

Julio Godoy

Julio Godoy, a native of Guatemala, now lives in Paris, France, where he has been the Inter Press Service correspondent since 1999. He is an award-winning journalist for his coverage of human rights violations in Guatemala, the international weapons trade, and the worldwide trend toward privatization of water.

In the following selection, Godoy reports that former French president Jacques Chirac and his political party tried to revise history by reframing French colonialism, especially in Algeria, as a positive thing. The Algerians were infuriated at this attempt to cover up the torture and other abuses inflicted by French forces during Algeria's war for independence in the late 1950s and early 1960s. According to Godoy, French historians and some senators denounced the Chirac plan, and teachers proclaimed they would not teach from textbooks that promoted false history.

France and other European countries are claiming, either officially or through historians, that colonialism was a positive thing.

In a law passed on Feb. 23 [2005], the French parliament, dominated by President Jacques Chirac's right-leaning Union for a Popular Movement (UMP), demanded that teachers at schools all over the country and textbooks emphasise "the positive role (played by) France overseas, especially in the Maghreb region" in North Africa.

This move sparked debate among French historians, politicians, teachers, and representatives of former colonies, especially Algeria.

Julio Godoy, "France: Recasting Colonialism as a Good Thing," *OneWorld.net*, July 6, 2005. Reproduced by permission.

At first, the Algerian government considered calling a special joint session of the two chambers of parliament to discuss the issue and formulate a response to the French claims.

But President Abdelaziz Bouteflika decided against the special session. Instead, the two chambers will review the issue separately and adopt a resolution condemning "the crimes of colonisation."

Algerians Object

While this official reaction comes against a backdrop of Algerian efforts to normalise relations with the former colonial power and a plan to sign a special co-operation agreement with Paris, Algeria's response to France's attempt to rewrite history shows that the wounds provoked by colonialism in the Maghreb are still sore.

On Jun. 7, [2005,] almost four months after the law was passed in Paris, the National Liberation Front (FLN), Algeria's ruling party, which evolved from the 1950s independence movement against France, released a communiqué in which it firmly condemned the French claims.

The French law, the FLN stated, "glorifies colonialism and a retrograde vision of history," and tries to justify "the barbarity of colonialism by erasing the most hideous acts" committed by French forces in Algeria.

The FLN statement was signed by Abdelaziz Belkhadem, minister for foreign affairs until May 1 [2005]. Belkhadem is considered to be the closest advisor to Bouteflika, who is himself honorary president of the governing party.

Bachir Boumaza, who fought in the Algerian war of independence in the late 1950s and was tortured by French forces, said too that the French law defending colonialism "is morally equivalent to efforts to rewrite the historical record of the Nazi regime in Germany."

Boumaza, whose book, *La Gangrene* ("The Gangrene"), described the torture methods employed by French colonial forces during the Algerian war, added that "praising colonialism, a system universally condemned, cannot contribute to curing the historical conflict it gave birth to."

"Colonialism is, above all, the humiliation of human beings," he said. "It is sad that France is not able to put an end to its colonialist mentality."

A Bloody War for Freedom

Algeria won independence from France in 1962 after a bloody eight-year war during which the French military employed the most brutal counterinsurgency methods. At the time, only a handful of French intellectuals, including philosopher Jean-Paul Sartre and historian Pierre Vidal Naquet, denounced French abuses in Algeria.

Together with journalist Claude Bourdet, editor of the weekly newspaper *France Observateur*, Vidal Naquet publicly compared the French forces' behaviour in Algeria to that of the Nazi Gestapo secret police.

In Paris, leftist parliamentarians, such as socialist senators Bariza Khiari and Jean-Pierre Michel, have called the new efforts by the French government to revise colonialism's historical record "a crime against memory."

French Law Denounced

In a joint declaration released in late June, [2005,] Khiari and Michel denounced the French law as "an unacceptable, unprecedented provocation, which insults the historical facts and the victims of colonialism alike, and also historians and researchers who have condemned colonialism."

Similar positions were adopted by historians and teachers. The French association of history and geography teachers dismissed the law as "a call to write an official version of history." History professor François Durpaire told IPS [Inter Press Service]: "It's as if the government had asked mathematicians to teach that two plus two equals five."

Durpaire and other history teachers and professors in France said, however, that the new law would certainly have no impact on the way history is taught in French schools, but that it merely forms part of an effort by France to cleanse its colonial past.

Historian Marc Ferro, author of "Le livre noir du colonialisme" (The Black Book of Colonialism), an uncompromising account of European colonialism, noted that France has always insisted on describing its own colonial practices as "humane," while dismissing British or Spanish colonialism as ruthless and inspired purely by the aim of economic domination.

"But in practice, the differences between French and English colonialism were not as clear-cut as the official French version would like them to be," Ferro told IPS. He added that French colonialism came to an abrupt end after World War II, provoking a new national crisis after the catastrophe of France's collaboration with Nazi Germany.

Meanwhile, British rule in Africa and Asia went, with the clear exceptions of India, Kenya, and Zimbabwe, through a smooth transition from colonialism to co-operation within the Commonwealth.

"We can say that if French cultural intentions were perhaps more humane than Britain's, France's political practices in the colonies were actually more restrictive and repressive, in part because colonial France wanted the indigenous peoples in the colonies to become French. Britain never thought of transforming Kenyans or Indians into Englishmen," Ferro added.

France's right-wing government is not alone in attempting to revise the colonial past. In Britain, historian Niall Ferguson has for years conveyed a revisionist view of colonialism, describing British colonial rule in Africa and Asia as "nation-building."

French president Jacques Chirac (right) greets Algerian president Abdelaziz Bouteflika upon his arrival at the Elysee Palace, in Paris, on June 14, 2000. Bouteflika was on an official visit seeking to put his official seal on a new era of relations between the two countries. AP Images.

Historian Urges U.S. Colonialism

Ferguson has said that the British empire succeeded in transforming "the institutions of failed or rogue states and lay the foundations of . . . rule of law, non-corrupt administration, and ultimately, representative government."

Among such "failed or rogue states" Ferguson included India.

He also claimed that the British empire succeeded in giving rise to a lengthy period of "relative world peace" and a global order within which economic development was unquestionably easier.

In addition, Ferguson has stated that poverty in Third World countries is not a product of colonialism or globalisation, but is rooted in the fact that those "areas of the world have no contact with globalisation. It's not globalisation that makes them poor, it's the fact that they're not involved in it."

In his latest works, especially in his book "*Colossus: The rise and Fall of the American Empire*", Ferguson, now a professor of history at Harvard University, has been calling on U.S. officials to aggressively assure their role as new colonial masters—as heirs to the British empire, so to speak.

He has even claimed that an "imperial gene" exists—which apparently would be of Anglo-Saxon origin.

These appeals have led other historians, curiously mainly in France, to dismiss Ferguson as a 21st century historian thinking in 19th century terms.

Says Pierre Grosser, professor of history at the French Institute of Political Studies in Paris: "It is astonishing seeing Ferguson arguing in favour of U.S.-led colonialism and imperialism based on the so-called lessons drawn from the experience of the British empire."

The First Woman Elected President in Africa Is Called a Neocolonialist

Kuumba Chi Nia

Kuumba Chi Nia is a contributor to the news agency Mathaba and the Online Journal. *He is also a businessman and organizer for Pan-Africanism, a movement to unite all Africans.*

In the following viewpoint, Nia asserts that Ellen Johnson Sirleaf, the first woman elected president of an African nation, promotes colonialism by aligning herself with the United States. Nia says that AFRICOM, a communication headquarters established by the United States in Africa, is merely a way for the United States to protect its access to Africa's oil and natural gas. According to Nia, Sirleaf is exploiting Liberia as did her predecessor, Charles Taylor.

Ellen Johnson Sirleaf ran for President with the campaign slogan—"All the men have failed Liberia; let's try a woman." She is known as Africa's "Iron Woman," who reduced corruption, increased government revenue, restored relations with international lenders, and launched a Truth and Reconciliation Commission.

In the midst of President Sirleaf's fame and "first time" recognition, it must be recognized that she is no better for Liberia than the former dictator President Charles Taylor of Liberia who currently is before the International Criminal Court on 11 counts that amount to crimes against humanity and corruption. Women can rule or hold a leadership position equal to men or better; nevertheless, the struggle for us is ideological in nature and particular to the leader.

Kuumba Chi Nia, "AFRICOM: Imperialism Neo-Colonialism and the Fight for African Resources," doublestandards.org, November 30, 2007. Reproduced by permission of the author.

Sirleaf Exploits Liberia

African heads of states are forging toward continental unity in the tradition of Dr. Kwame Nkrumah, Sekou Ture, Tinia Sila, Tedora Gomes, Amil Cabral (Abdet Djassi) and other revolutionary Pan-Africanists. Non-alignment [with the United States] is essential for the independence of Africa. However, Sirleaf is attempting to align herself and Liberia with U.S. imperialism and ever since the 1800s and the "Back To Africa" movement the U.S. and Liberia have remained aligned in one form or the other. There is danger in this partnership. This partnership moves along the lines of slave-master relationship or exploiter and the exploited.

In his book *Neo-colonialism: The Last Stage of Imperialism*, Nkrumah spelled out the problems with imperialist intervention through finance capital and military occupation. That is why it is a stab in the back of all Pan-Africanists and to the Pan-African movement to witness the first woman elected president in Africa—Ellen Johnson Sirleaf—become the first African woman neo-colonialist. She follows the path of the former Liberian president Charles Taylor and former US puppet Samuel Doe. . . .

Sirleaf Government Allows Corruption

The United States established a base in Liberia during World War II, coupled with [multinational corporation] Firestone gaining land concessions to exploit the labor and raw materials that were used for U.S. military hardware and for other motor vehicle needs. Firestone remains in Liberia amidst a battle against the corporation for deplorable labor treatment especially the exploitation of children slave workers. The Sirleaf government is inept and allows it to continue. This vicious cycle of puppet prerogative, imperialist exploitation, and mass denigration must be challenged and stopped by any means necessary.

If Sirleaf loved the masses of Africa well enough, and Liberians in particular, then she would be an advocate for one military true enough, but an African High Command akin to Nkrumah's vision in the *Handbook of Revolutionary Warfare*. In addition she would call for strengthening the African Union and its military so that Africa can secure its own land and people.

The revolutionary leader Amil Cabral clearly pointed out the dilemma of neo-colonialists and simply put it as their *lack of a revolutionary consciousness*, echoing [Cuban] President Fidel Castro. . . .

U.S. Access to Oil

Cabral's words 41-years ago are compatible with neo-colonialism in the 21st century AD. Ryan Henry, principal [U.S.] Defense Department undersecretary for policy told reporters the purpose of AFRICOM [Africa Command] is not waging war, but "to work in concert with our African partners for a more stable environment in which political and economic growth can take place." In the same breath he skillfully bites his tongue and slightly dances around the true reason for wanting to establish a base in Africa, it is in concert with the rich deposits of oil and natural gas in Africa. Henry propagated the idea that economic development for the West African region is an aspect of the high command, and that in other words means Liberia and West Africa are ripe for the pickings. Liberia represents a historical ally that the U.S. relied upon even through the 14-year war and the U.S. keeps its eyes on the prize—oil.

The U.S. consumes nearly 20 million barrels of oil, with last year [2006], 22 percent of that oil imported from Africa. That was an increase of 7 percent from 2004. The National Intelligence Council projects that Africa will account for 25 percent by 2015, a staggering percentage amount from a continent that is in abject poverty, and the masses will suffer from not having electricity to study, wash dishes, bathe, and cook or provide their homes with the security of a well lit porch light. Several other countries are on the horizon for the oil exploitation and they are Ghana (currently talking about a U.S. military base), Angola and Equatorial Guinea. ExxonMobil and Chevron, France's Total and British Petroleum and Royal Dutch Shell will invest billions of dollars in Africa in the coming years. The cash cow Nigeria became the third largest exporter of oil to the U.S. in 2007, outstripping Saudi Arabia.

Sirleaf Offered Territory for U.S. Military

According to a report from Monrovia, Liberia, date July 6 [2007], on July 4th at a reception "marking the 231st Independence Anniversary of the United States", President Sirleaf said "Liberia, the U.S. historic ally, has stood resolutely with the United States, through good times and bad, and is offering its territory as it has done in the past, for the establishment of AFRICOM headquarters."

Chief Executive [George W.] Bush indicated that historical and strategic reasons make Liberia an ideal location for this important American initiative that will undoubtedly have a most beneficial effect on the West African sub-region, as well as the entire continent.

President Sirleaf welcomed the new United States policy towards Africa's security and development as reflected in the proposed establishment of a new Africa Command (AFRICOM).

If this puppet regime and Sirleaf believe that the U.S. is a friend of Africa then they are sadly mistaken and the helm is essentially the same as the former dictator Charles Taylor and puppet Samuel Doe before him who died naked on the floor and begging, once the African masses caught up with him. President Sirleaf would do well to wash her hands of U.S. imperialism and reject any attempt to further the cause of neo-colonialism in Africa. The resources of Liberia make it an attractive country to predators.

The United Nations Wants to Force Liberation on Unwilling Colonies

Ian Mather

Ian Mather is a British journalist who, in 1982, was imprisoned in Argentina for nearly three months for reporting on the Falklands War between Great Britain and Argentina.

In the following viewpoint, Mather states that the United Nations declared colonialism "an anachronism in the 21st century" and sought to decolonize the world's sixteen remaining colonies. That group includes the U.S. territories of the Virgin Islands, Guam, and American Samoa. One colony, Tokelau, a tiny island administered by New Zealand, did not want independence. Mather quotes decolonization critics who said that diplomats were embarrassed that colonies remained in the twenty-first century. Like Tokelau, most of the existing colonies are too small to function independently and still remain viable. A February 2006 referendum on self-governance was defeated by Tokelau voters.

As if its role in Iraq were not onerous enough, the United Nations is seeking to impose "regime change" on a tiny speck of land in the Pacific Ocean.

The territory of Tokelau lies halfway between New Zealand and Hawaii, and consists of three atolls with a total area of seven square miles. Its resident population of 1,500 travel to the outside world by an occasional visiting ship.

Yet it is on the UN's list of the world's 16 remaining colonies, and the UN has sworn to make it independent whether its inhabitants like it or not.

Ian Mather, "UN Cries Freedom to Contented Colonies," *Scotland on Sunday*, May 23, 2004. Reproduced by permission.

This week [of May 23, 2004,] the UN launches a week of "Solidarity with the Peoples of Non-Self-governing Territories" in a drive to "liberate" them.

Five are in the Pacific, where last week the UN held a conference to draw attention to their plight, with Tokelau at the top of the agenda.

Not Interested in Being a Microstate

However, the Tokelauans, a Polynesian people, are reluctant over any change in status which would create the world's ultimate microstate. It has no capital or airport, and more of its population live outside its borders than on its territory, since thousands of Tokelauans live in New Zealand, which controls Tokelau.

Last week, the leader of Tokelau challenged plans by the UN and New Zealand to make the territory hold a referendum on self-determination.

"For Tokelau, the most important thing in the decolonisation process is that the people of Tokelau, the elders, the fishermen, the weavers, the young children, know what it means," Patuki Isa'ako told the meeting in Mandang, Papua New Guinea. "Otherwise, we're just wasting our time.

"Why would we want to declare to the international community we have self-determination? While we may work on intangibles such as pride of the people, pride of being self-determined, we've always asked the question, what's it for? Is it going to feed our mouths? Is it going to feed our children? What good is it for future generations?"

However, the UN is undeterred in its drive to get Tokelau to hold a vote. Describing colonialism as "an anachronism in the 21st century" UN Secretary General Kofi Annan told the conference: "Decolonisation is a UN success story but it is a story that is not yet finished. We must see the process through to its end."

New Zealand Unhappy Being on List

Critics claim that New Zealand, which strongly lobbied for French decolonisation in the Pacific, is embarrassed to be on the UN's list of states that administer colonies.

"They want to make Tokelau independent because to some diplomats it is embarrassing to have the UN going there now and again and inspecting the place," said one insider, who did not want to be named.

More than 80 nations formerly under colonial rule have become independent since the UN was formed in 1945.

"The decolonisation efforts of the United Nations derive from the principle of equal rights and self-determination of peoples," the UN says.

But the problem for UN purists is that most of the colonies are either too small to be viable, or are populated by people who do not want to be independent.

The 16 remaining colonies are mostly in the Caribbean or the Pacific. In addition to Tokelau the UN list includes the US territories of the Virgin Islands, Guam and American Samoa; the British territories of Anguilla, Bermuda, British Virgin Islands, Cayman Islands, Falkland Islands, Gibraltar, Montserrat, Pitcairn Island, St Helena and the Turks and Caicos Islands; the French territory of New Caledonia; and Morocco's Western Sahara.

Most could not function without hefty subsidies from the administering countries.

Right to Self-Determination

Three British dependent territories, the Falkland Islands, Gibraltar and Bermuda are exceptional in that they are economically sound.

The Falkland Islanders have become wealthy through fish, and the Gibraltarians through finance and tourism, while the 65,000-strong population of Bermuda enjoys one of the highest living standards in the world.

Men carry a ballot box for Tokelau's 2006 referendum on whether it should become independent from New Zealand. David Brooks/AFP/Getty Images.

Gibraltar and the Falkland Islands have the right to self-determination enshrined in their constitutions. But, unlike the UN, both argue that the right to self-determination should include the right to protection from other nations with claims on the territory.

In two referendums the people of Gibraltar have rejected the transfer of sovereignty to Spain and the sharing of sovereignty between Britain and Spain.

The Falkland Islanders are unanimously opposed to being taken over by Argentina.

In Bermuda there is disagreement among the parties over independence. [In 2004] prime minister Alex Scott backed the UN's call for decolonisation. He said that the Progressive Labour Party (PLP) had long favoured independence "and that position has not changed".

But opposition leader Grant Gibbons said that the UN had no business "telling the people of Bermuda what's good for us. We are a sophisticated and mature people and it's a matter for Bermudians to decide when and how we wish to move to independence".

For Further Discussion

1. In Chapter 1, Romanus Okey Muoneke's viewpoint explains how, in African cultures, art and society are inseparable. Achebe has stated that he feels duty-bound, as an African writer, to educate about and influence African political and social issues, particularly in Nigeria. How do you perceive the role of artists in the United States or other countries you are familiar with? Do you think all artists have a responsibility to speak out about their views and try to influence or persuade others? Why or why not? Can you identify any artists who use their fame to promote their political or social views?

2. In Chapter 2 Ada Uzoamaka Azodo points out that the males in *Things Fall Apart*, both the Igbo and the colonizers, use language to establish their status and power. They use speech patterns, as well as words, to convey their dominance. What words or phrases of dialogue do you think were most powerful in the novel? Thinking about male authority figures you are familiar with, do they use certain words or ways of speaking that establish their position? Do women in positions of power also use language in this manner?

3. In writing *Things Fall Apart* more than fifty years ago, Achebe wanted to dispel the many inaccurate perceptions of African culture and people by telling the story from the Igbo people's point of view, instead of the prevailing Eurocentric perspective. Do you think stereotypes about Africa and Africans are still prevalent in Western nations such as the United States? Have you or people you know experienced stereotyping? How have you or others dealt with the situation?

4. Umelo Ojinmah in Chapter 2 promotes the view that Okonkwo's tragedy was of his own making because he abused his position of power and responsibility within the Igbo society. Willene P. Taylor states that, as the novel concludes, Okonkwo is alone in defending his society's values against Western influences. Do you think that Okonkwo is a noble character in his unswerving dedication to the ways of his people and that the odds were against him? Or was he flawed, too angry and bull-headed, and unwilling to change with the times? What considerations or elements of the novel helped you arrive at your opinion?

5. Colonialism has been a theme throughout recorded history. In Chapter 3, John A. Burton and Stanley Douglas Stych believe that colonialism still exists in various forms throughout the world—as foreign aid, in using other nations' land for food production, and via programs to distribute laptops to children in developing countries. Do you agree with their conclusions that the "receiving" nations are being exploited? Why or why not? Do you think colonialism is an inevitable outcome of economic disparities between developed and developing countries? Explain your answer.

For Further Reading

Chinua Achebe, *Anthills of the Savannah*. London: Heinemann, 1987.

———, *Arrow of God*. London: Heinemann, 1964.

———, *Beware, Soul Brother, and Other Poems*. Enugu, Nigeria: Nwankwo-Ifejika, 1971.

———, *Chike and the River*. Cambridge: Cambridge University Press, 1966.

———, *Girls at War and Other Stories*. London: Heinemann, 1972.

———, *Home and Exile*. Oxford: Oxford University Press, 2000.

———, *A Man of the People*. London: Heinemann, 1966.

———, *No Longer at Ease*. London: Heinemann, 1960.

———, *The Sacrificial Egg, and Other Short Stories*. Onitsha, Nigeria: Etudo, 1962.

———, *The Trouble with Nigeria*. Enugu, Nigeria: Fourth Dimension, 1983.

Joseph Conrad, *Heart of Darkness*. London: Dent & Sons, 1902.

Daniel Defoe, *Robinson Crusoe*. London: W. Taylor, 1719.

Rudyard Kipling, *Kim*. London: MacMillan, 1901.

Pramoedya Ananta Toer, *This Earth of Mankind*. Trans. Max Lane. New York: Penguin, 1981.

Bibliography

Books

John Agetua, ed.   *Critics on Chinua Achebe, 1970–76.* Benin City, Nigeria: Agetua, 1977.

Marwan Bishara   *Palestine/Israel: Peace or Apartheid; Occupation, Terrorism and the Future.* Rev. ed. London and New York: Zed Books, 2003.

M. Keith Booker, ed.   *The Chinua Achebe Encyclopedia.* Westport, CT: Heinemann Educational Books, 2003.

David Carroll   *Chinua Achebe.* New York: Twayne, 1970.

Herbert M. Cole and Chike Cyril Aniakor   *Igbo Arts: Community and Cosmos.* Los Angeles: Museum of Cultural History, University of California, 1984.

Prema Kumari Dheram   *Deprogramming Through Cultural Nationalism: Achebe and Ellison.* Delhi, India: B.R., 1994.

William Easterly   *The White Man's Burden: Why the West's Efforts to Aid the Rest Have Done So Much Ill and So Little Good.* New York: Penguin, 2006.

Ernest Emenyonu   *The Rise of the Igbo Novel.* Ibadan, Nigeria: Oxford University Press, 1978.

Ezenwa-Ohaeto	*Chinua Achebe: A Biography.* Bloomington: Indiana University Press, 1997.
Shatto Arthur Gakwandi	*The Novel and Contemporary Experience in Africa.* London: Heinemann; New York: Africana, 1977.
Simon Gikandi	*Reading Achebe.* London: Currey, 1991.
Michael Harris	*Outsiders and Insiders: Perspectives of Third World Culture in British and Post-Colonial Fiction.* New York: Peter Lang, 1994.
David Harvey	*The New Imperialism.* New York: Oxford University Press, 2005.
Catherine Lynette Innes	*Chinua Achebe.* Cambridge: Cambridge University Press, 1990.
Christophe Tshikala Kambaji	*Chinua Achebe: A Novelist and a Portraitist of His Society.* New York: Vantage, 1994.
Sidney Lens	*The Forging of the American Empire, from the Revolution to Vietnam: A History of U.S. Imperialism.* New ed. London: Pluto, 2003.
Bernth Lindfors	*Conversations with Chinua Achebe.* Jackson: University Press of Mississippi, 1997.
Isidore Okpewho	*Chinua Achebe's "Things Fall Apart": A Casebook.* New York: Oxford University Press, 2003.

Raisa Simola   *World Views in Chinua Achebe's Works*. New York: Peter Lang, 1995.

Florence Stratton   *Contemporary African Literature and the Politics of Gender*. New York: Routledge, 1994.

Oladele Taiwo   *Culture and the Nigerian Novel*. London: MacMillan, 1976.

Robert M. Wren   *Achebe's World: The Historical and Cultural Context of the Novels of Chinua Achebe*. Washington, DC: Three Continents, 1980.

Periodicals

Tunji Adebayo   "The Past and the Present in Chinua Achebe's Novels," *Ife African Studies*, March 1974.

Toyin   *"Things Fall Apart* at 40," *Glendora*
Adewale-Gabriel   *Review: African Quarterly on the Arts*, vol. 2, no. 3, 1998.

Roger Bowen   "Speaking Truth to Power: An Interview with Chinua Achebe," *Academe*, January/February 2005.

Arun Gupta   "Slumdog Colonialism: Hollywood Mines Another Culture for Raw Material, Celebrates a Box-Office Bonanza," *The Indypendent*, March 20, 2009.

Abiola Irele et al.   "Chinua Achebe at Seventy," *Research in African Literatures*, Fall 2001.

Abdul-Rasheed Na'Allah	"Postcolonial Nigeria, African Literature and the Twenty-first Century: An Interview with Chinua Achebe," *Neohelicon*, January 1999.
Merun Nasser	"Achebe and His Women: A Social Science Perspective," *Africa Today*, vol. 3, 1980.
Robert H. Nelson	"Environmental Colonialism: 'Saving' Africa from Africans," *The Independent Review*, Summer 2003.
Molara Ogundipe-Leslie	"Nigeria, Alienation and the Novels of Chinua Achebe," *Black World*, June 1973.
Clement Abiaziem Okafor	"A Sense of History in the Novels of Chinua Achebe," *Journal of African Studies*, Summer 1981.
Kwadwo Opoku-Agyemang	"A Crisis of Balance: The (Mis)representation of Colonial History and the Slave Experience as Themes in Modern African Literature," *Okike: An African Journal of New Writing*, February 1996.
Diana Akers Rhoads	"Culture in Chinua Achebe's *Things Fall Apart*," *African Studies Review*, September 1993.
Mark Anthony Rolo	"Re-remembering Christopher Columbus on Columbus Day," *The Progressive*, October 12, 2009.

Bob Thompson   "Things Fall Into Place; Chinua
                  Achebe Remembers How He Came
                  to Be the Father of Modern African
                  Literature," *Washington Post*, March
                  9, 2008.

Internet Sources

L. Chinedu   "AFRICOM and Modern Day
Arizona-Ogwu   Colonialism: The Precaution Yar'
                  Adua Should Take," *Nigerians in
                  America*, December 22, 2007.
                  www.nigeriansinamerica.com.

Vinicius Valentin "Colonialism and Underdevelopment
Raduan Miguel   in Latin America," *PoliticalAffairs*,
                   August 3, 2009.
                   www.politicalaffairs.net.

Yoginder Sikand   "Christian Supremacists and
                  American Imperialism,"
                  Countercurrents.org, October 28,
                  2006. www.countercurrents.org.

Index

flaws in, 25–26, 49–50, 54–55, 83–84
proverb use by, 63–64
rejection of, by Okomkwo, 55–56, 84, 90–91
U.S. colonialism, 137–138
The Uses of African Literature (Achebe), 42

V

Violence
of Okonkwo, 47–51, 56–59, 73, 85
against women, 56, 74–76
Voice of Nigeria, 23

W

Welch, James, 31
Western literature, depiction of Africa in, 11, 21, 24, 71–72
Western values, 121–122
Women
child-bearing role of, 73–74
in *Things Fall Apart*, 71–79
violence against, 56, 74–76
Writer, role of, 37–39, 42–45, 61

Y

Yeats, William Butler, 33, 88–89, 103